D0985548

TO:

_____

FROM:

_____

DATE:

_____

POCKETFUL OF
Bible Promises
FOR
GODLY LEADERS

LIVE YOUR FAITH

Bible Translations Used:

HCSB: Scripture quotations marked HCSB®, are taken from the Holman Christian Standard Bible®, Copyright © 1999, 2000, 2002, 2003, 2009 by Holman Bible Publishers. Used by permission. HCSB® is a federally registered trademark of Holman Bible Publishers.

ICB: Scripture taken from The Holy Bible, International Children's Bible® Copyright© 1986, 1988, 1999, 2015 by Tommy Nelson™, a division of Thomas Nelson. Used by permission.

KJV: Scripture taken from The Holy Bible, King James Version.

NASB: Scripture quotations taken from the New American Standard Bible®, Copyright © 1960, 1962, 1963, 1968, 1971, 1972, 1973, 1975, 1977, 1995 by The Lockman Foundation Used by permission.

NCV: Scripture taken from the New Century Version. Copyright © 1987, 1988, 1991 by Thomas Nelson, Inc. Used by permission. All rights reserved.

NIV: Scripture quotations marked (NIV) are taken from the Holy Bible, New International Version®, NIV®. Copyright © 1973, 1978, 1984, 2011 by Biblica, Inc.™ Used by permission of Zondervan. All rights reserved worldwide. www.zondervan.com The "NIV" and "New International Version" are trademarks registered in the United States Patent and Trademark Office by Biblica, Inc.™

NKJV: Scripture taken from the New King James Version. Copyright © 1982 by Thomas Nelson, Inc. Used by permission. All rights reserved.

NLT: Holy Bible, New Living Translation, copyright © 1996, 2004, 2015 by Tyndale House Foundation. Used by permission of Tyndale House Publishers, Inc. All rights reserved.

MSG: Scripture taken from The Message. Copyright © 1993, 1994, 1995, 1996, 2000, 2001, 2002. Used by permission of NavPress Publishing Group.

Cover design by Jessica Wei

ISBN: 978-1-68408-112-7

CONTENTS

INTRODUCTION

In your hands you hold a simple, Biblically based guidebook for men and women who seek to serve their Creator in capacities of leadership. How desperately our world needs servant-leaders who humbly honor God while following in the footsteps of His Son. If you're willing to assume that responsibility, the ideas on these pages are sure to help.

The Bible is a book like no other. It is a gift from the Creator, an instruction book for life here on earth and a roadmap for life eternal. And it's a book of promises.

When God makes a promise, He keeps it. No exceptions. So the verses in this text are not hypotheticals; they're certainties. They apply to every generation, including yours, and they apply to every human being, including you.

God has a plan for your life and He will provide every tool you need to accomplish His will. But that's not all. He also offers eternal love and eternal life. And that's a promise that you can depend on, now and forever.

1

ACTION

But prove yourselves doers of the word,
and not merely hearers who delude themselves.
JAMES 1:22 NASB

When something needs to be done, the best time to do it is now, not later. But we're tempted to do otherwise. When the task at hand is difficult or unpleasant, we're tempted to procrastinate. But procrastination is the enemy of progress and a stumbling block on the path to success.

So, if you'd like to jumpstart your career or your life, ask God to give you the strength and the wisdom to do first things first, even if the first thing is hard. And while you're at it, use this time-tested formula for success: Employ less talk and more action. Why? Because actions indeed speak louder than words—always have, always will. And a thousand good intentions pale in comparison to a single good deed.

Action springs not from thought,
but from a readiness for responsibility.
DIETRICH BONHOEFFER

GOD'S PROMISES
ABOUT TAKING ACTION NOW

For the kingdom of God
is not a matter of talk but of power.
1 CORINTHIANS 4:20 HCSB

Therefore, with your minds ready for action,
be serious and set your hope completely
on the grace to be brought to you
at the revelation of Jesus Christ.
1 PETER 1:13 HCSB

Whenever we have the opportunity,
we should do good to everyone,
especially to those in the family of faith.
GALATIANS 6:10 NLT

When you make a vow to God,
do not delay to fulfill it.
He has no pleasure in fools; fulfill your vow.
ECCLESIASTES 5:4 NIV

Well done, good and faithful servant;
you were faithful over a few things,
I will make you ruler over many things.
Enter into the joy of your lord.
MATTHEW 25:21 NKJV

2

ADVERSITY

We are hard-pressed on every side, yet not crushed;
we are perplexed, but not in despair.
2 CORINTHIANS 4:8 NKJV

The times that try men's souls are also the times when character is forged on the anvil of adversity. But the character building is never easy. Surviving tough times requires courage, strength, prayer, and plenty of hard work.

During difficult times, we are tempted to complain, to worry, to blame, and to do little else. Usually, complaints and worries change nothing; intelligent work, on the other hand, changes everything for the better.

When times are tough, even the most dedicated men and women are tempted to lose hope. But we must never abandon our hopes altogether. And we must never stop trusting God, who never gives us heavier burdens than we can bear.

If we are to build better lives for ourselves and our loved ones, we must continue to believe in— and work for—a brighter future. We must not give in; we must persevere. What's required is a combination of faith, work, wisdom, courage, and determination. When we face our challenges with open eyes, courageous hearts, plenty of prayer, and willing hands, miracles happen.

When life kicks you, let it kick you forward.
E. STANLEY JONES

GOD'S PROMISES
ABOUT ADVERSITY

I called to the LORD in my distress; I called to my God.
From His temple He heard my voice.
2 SAMUEL 22:7 HCSB

The LORD is my rock, my fortress, and my deliverer,
my God, my mountain where I seek refuge.
My shield, the horn of my salvation,
my stronghold, my refuge, and my Savior.
2 SAMUEL 22:2–3 HCSB

God blesses those who patiently endure testing
and temptation. Afterward they will
receive the crown of life that God
has promised to those who love him.
JAMES 1:12 NLT

He heals the brokenhearted
and binds up their wounds.
PSALM 147:3 HCSB

The LORD is my shepherd; I shall not want.
PSALM 23:1 KJV

3

ADVICE: GIVING IT

Good people's words will help many others.

PROVERBS 10:21 NCV

Wise leaders know how and when to dispense advice. From experience, they know the right thing to say and the right way to say it. Sometimes the message can be delivered softly; on other occasions, more direct communication is needed. While leadership styles vary, Christian leaders are instructed—and constrained—by the teachings and commandments found in God's holy Word.

The Bible teaches that we must treat others in the same way that we wish to be treated: with dignity, respect, compassion, and concern. That's how leaders should treat their coworkers.

Today, as you fulfill your duties, consider what it means to be a Christian communicator. Be clear *and* compassionate. Choose your words carefully, and don't say anything to another human being that you wouldn't say if Jesus were standing right by your side...because He is.

The true secret of giving advice is, after you've given it, to be perfectly indifferent whether it is taken or not.
HANNAH WHITALL SMITH

GOD'S PROMISES
ABOUT GIVING ADVICE

Let the wise listen and add to their learning,
and let the discerning get guidance.
PROVERBS 1:5 NIV

Wise people can also listen and learn.
PROVERBS 1:5 NCV

The wise store up knowledge,
but the mouth of the fool hastens destruction.
PROVERBS 10:14 HCSB

Walk with the wise and become wise;
associate with fools and get in trouble.
PROVERBS 13:20 NLT

How much better to get wisdom
than gold! And to get understanding
is to be chosen rather than silver.
PROVERBS 16:16 NKJV

4

ADVICE: TAKING IT

The wise are glad to be instructed.
PROVERBS 10:8 NLT

Every leader, no matter how wise, needs advisors. We live in a world that is so complicated and so complex that no one is wise enough by himself. We all need trusted counselors to help us think clearly, plan wisely, and implement our plans at the right time, in the right way.

Wise leaders seek counsel from a variety of sources. They are constantly searching for ways to make things better, and they're not afraid of contrary opinions or constructive criticism. In fact, they seek a wide spectrum of ideas, always aware that group-think and popular opinions are often wrong.

So, the next time you're faced with a difficult decision, start by talking things over with God, but don't stop there. As the old saying goes, two heads are, indeed, better than one. And sometimes three are better than two. And on occasion four are better than...well, you get the idea.

Don't be afraid to take advice.
There's always something new to learn.
BABE RUTH

GOD'S PROMISES
ABOUT TAKING ADVICE

*How much better is it to get wisdom
than gold! and to get understanding
rather to be chosen than silver!*
PROVERBS 16:16 KJV

*Plans fail when there is no counsel,
but with many advisers they succeed.*
PROVERBS 15:22 HCSB

*He whose ear listens to the life-giving reproof
will dwell among the wise.*
PROVERBS 15:31 NASB

*Get all the advice and instruction you can,
so you will be wise the rest of your life.*

PROVERBS 19:20 NLT

5

ANGER

Everyone must be quick to hear,
slow to speak, and slow to anger, for man's anger
does not accomplish God's righteousness.
JAMES 1:19–20 HCSB

Wise leaders understand—and the Bible promises—that patience pays and anger costs. Anger is harmful, hurtful, and hazardous to your spiritual health, but in the heat of the battle, you'll be tempted to lose your temper. Hopefully you'll learn to resist that temptation.

Whenever your thoughts are hijacked by angry emotions, you forfeit the peace and perspective that might otherwise be yours. And to make matters worse, angry thoughts may cause you to behave in irrational, self-destructive ways. As the old saying goes, "Anger is only one letter away from danger."

First Peter 5:8–9 warns, "Stay alert! Watch out for your great enemy, the devil. He prowls around like a roaring lion, looking for someone to devour. Stand firm against him, and be strong in your faith" (NLT). And of this you can be sure: Your adversary will use an impatient and unforgiving heart—and the inevitable anger that dwells within it—to sabotage your life and undermine your faith. To be safe, you must cleanse your heart, and you must forgive. You must say yes to God, yes to mercy, yes to love, yes to patience, and no to anger.

Anger and bitterness—whatever the cause—
only end up hurting us. Turn that anger over to Christ.
BILLY GRAHAM

GOD'S PROMISES
ABOUT ANGER

But I tell you that anyone who is angry
with his brother or sister will be subject to judgment.
MATTHEW 5:22 NIV

He who is slow to wrath has great understanding,
but he who is impulsive exalts folly.
PROVERBS 14:29 NKJV

A hot-tempered man stirs up conflict,
but a man slow to anger calms strife.
PROVERBS 15:18 HCSB

But now you must also put away all the following:
anger, wrath, malice, slander,
and filthy language from your mouth.
COLOSSIANS 3:8 HCSB

Do not let the sun go down on your anger,
and do not give the devil an opportunity.
EPHESIANS 4:26–27 NASB

6

ANXIETY
AND WORRY

Therefore do not worry about tomorrow,
for tomorrow will worry about its own things.
Sufficient for the day is its own trouble.
MATTHEW 6:34 NKJV

Because we are human beings who have the capacity to think and to anticipate future events, we worry. We worry about big things, little things, and just about everything in between. To make matters worse, we live in a world that breeds anxiety and fosters fear. So it's not surprising that when we come face to face with tough times, we may fall prey to discouragement, doubt, or depression. But our Father in heaven has other plans.

Even the most confident leaders are plagued by the inevitable worries that accompany responsibility. But God has promised that we can lead lives of abundance, not anxiety. In fact, His Word instructs us to "be anxious for nothing" (Philippians 4:6 NKJV). So how can we put our fears to rest? By taking those fears to Him and leaving them there.

The very same God who created the universe has promised to protect you now and forever. So what do you have to worry about? With God on your side, the answer is "nothing."

Knowing that God is faithful,
it really helps me to not be captivated by worry.
JOSH MCDOWELL

GOD'S PROMISES
ABOUT ANXIETY AND WORRY

Let not your heart be troubled;
you believe in God, believe also in Me.
JOHN 14:1 NKJV

Cast all your anxiety on him because he cares for you.
1 PETER 5:7 NIV

Peace I leave with you; My peace I give to you;
not as the world gives do I give to you.
Do not let your heart be troubled, nor let it be fearful.
JOHN 14:27 NASB

Do not be anxious about anything,
but in everything, by prayer and petition,
with thanksgiving, present your requests to God.
PHILIPPIANS 4:6 NIV

Cast your burden on the LORD,
And He shall sustain you;
He shall never permit the righteous to be moved.
PSALM 55:22 NKJV

7

ASKING GOD

Ask, and it shall be given to you; seek, and you shall find; knock, and it shall be opened to you. For every one who asks receives, and he who seeks finds, and to him who knocks it will be opened.

MATTHEW 7:7–8 NASB

The Lord invites us to pray about the things we need, and He promises to hear our prayers. God is always available and He's always ready to help us. And He knows precisely what we need, but He still instructs us to ask.

Do you make a habit of asking God for the things you need? Hopefully so. After all, the Father most certainly has a plan for your life. And He can do great things through you if you have the courage to ask for His guidance and His help. So be fervent in prayer and don't hesitate to ask the Creator for the tools you need to accomplish His plan for your life. Then, get busy and expect the best. When you do your part, God will most certainly do His part. And great things are bound to happen.

We honor God by asking for great things when they are a part of His promise. We dishonor Him and cheat ourselves when we ask for molehills where He has promised mountains.

VANCE HAVNER

GOD'S PROMISES
ABOUT ASKING HIM

Until now you have asked for nothing in My name.
Ask and you will receive,
so that your joy may be complete.
JOHN 16:24 HCSB

Do not be anxious about anything,
but in every situation, by prayer and petition,
with thanksgiving, present your requests to God.
PHILIPPIANS 4:6 NIV

The effective prayer of a righteous man
can accomplish much.
JAMES 5:16 NASB

Your Father knows the things
you have need of before you ask Him.
MATTHEW 6:8 NKJV

You did not choose me, but I chose you
and appointed you to go and bear fruit—
fruit that will last—and so that whatever
you ask in my name the Father will give you.
JOHN 15:16 NIV

8

ATTITUDE

Finally, brothers, rejoice. Become mature,
be encouraged, be of the same mind, be at peace,
and the God of love and peace will be with you.
2 CORINTHIANS 13:11 HCSB

For leaders, attitude determines altitude; those with can-do attitudes rise to the top, while the naysayers sink.

Attitudes are the mental filters through which we view and interpret the world around us. Your attitude will inevitably determine the quality and direction of your day, your career, and your life. That's why it's so important to stay positive.

The Christian life can be, and should be, cause for celebration. After all, every new day is a gift, every new circumstance an opportunity to praise and to serve. So what's your attitude today? Are you expecting God to do big things in your life and your organization? Are you willing to work hard, work smart, and encourage your coworkers to do likewise? Will you lead the way for others? Will you put down stepping stones, not stumbling blocks? If so, your efforts will be rewarded, perhaps sooner than you think.

It's easy to have a great attitude when things are going
our way. It's when difficult challenges rise before us
that attitude becomes the difference maker.
JOHN MAXWELL

GOD'S PROMISES
ABOUT ATTITUDE

A merry heart makes a cheerful countenance....
PROVERBS 15:13 NKJV

*You must have the same attitude
that Christ Jesus had.*
PHILIPPIANS 2:5 NLT

*Be glad and rejoice,
because your reward is great in heaven.*
MATTHEW 5:12 HCSB

Rejoice always; pray without ceasing.
1 THESSALONIANS 5:16–17 NASB

*This is the day the LORD has made;
let us rejoice and be glad in it.*
PSALM 118:24 HCSB

9

BEGINNING

Do not remember the former things, nor consider the things of old. Behold, I will do a new thing.
ISAIAH 43:18–19 NKJV

Sometimes the hardest thing to do is to begin. We have high hopes, big dreams, and grand plans. But somehow we never manage to move from the planning stage to the action stage. Meanwhile, as we play it safe and wait for the "perfect" time to start, the clock continues to tick as days turn into weeks, then months, then years.

Do you have an exciting plan that you haven't yet acted upon? Are you playing it safe, perhaps too safe, by waiting for the ideal moment to begin? If so, you may be missing important opportunities.

Oswald Chambers observed, "The one word in the spiritual vocabulary is now." But sometimes, because we're uncertain or afraid, we give in to our fears and we manufacture reasons for delay. To do so is unwise. Procrastination can be expensive, sometimes very expensive. So if you've been putting off your next grand adventure, it's probably time to reorder your to-do list. The best day to begin an important task is this day. Tomorrow, or the next day, or the next, may be too late.

God specializes in giving people a fresh start.
RICK WARREN

GOD'S PROMISES
ABOUT BEGINNING

Your old sinful self has died,
and your new life is kept with Christ in God.
COLOSSIANS 3:3 NCV

You are being renewed in the spirit of your minds; you
put on the new self, the one created according to God's
likeness in righteousness and purity of the truth.
EPHESIANS 4:23–24 HCSB

There is one thing I always do. Forgetting the past and
straining toward what is ahead, I keep trying to reach
the goal and get the prize for which God called me....
PHILIPPIANS 3:13–14 NCV

Then the One seated on the throne said,
"Look! I am making everything new."
REVELATION 21:5 HCSB

"For I know the plans I have for you"—
this is the LORD's declaration—"plans for your welfare,
not for disaster, to give you a future and a hope."
JEREMIAH 29:11 HCSB

10

BEHAVIOR

Now by this we know that we know Him,
if we keep His commandments.
1 JOHN 2:3 NKJV

It's always been true: actions, indeed, speak louder than words. No matter how loudly we proclaim our love for the Lord, our actions reveal our true priorities. As Thomas Fuller observed, "He does not believe who does not live according to his beliefs."

Every day, we make decisions that can bring us closer to God, or not. When we follow closely in the footsteps of Christ, we experience His abundance and His peace. But when we stray far from God's path, we bring needless pain and suffering upon ourselves and our families.

Do you want to experience God's peace and His blessings? Then obey Him. When you do, you will be blessed today, and tomorrow, and forever.

Resolved, never to do anything which I would be
afraid to do if it were the last hour of my life.
JONATHAN EDWARDS

GOD'S PROMISES
ABOUT BEHAVIOR

Walk in a manner worthy of the God
who calls you into His own kingdom and glory.
1 THESSALONIANS 2:12 NASB

Live peaceful and quiet lives
in all godliness and holiness.
1 TIMOTHY 2:2 NIV

But prove yourselves doers of the word,
and not merely hearers who delude themselves.
JAMES 1:22 NASB

To do evil is like sport to a fool,
but a man of understanding has wisdom.
PROVERBS 10:23 NKJV

In everything set them an example
by doing what is good.
TITUS 2:7 NIV

11

BELIEFS

I have come as a light into the world, that whoever believes in Me should not abide in darkness.
JOHN 12:46 NKJV

Talking about our beliefs is easy; living by them is considerably harder. Yet God warns us that speaking about faith is not enough; we must also live by faith. Simply put, our theology must be demonstrated, not only with words but, more importantly, with actions.

As Christians, our instructions are clear: We should trust God's plan, obey God's Word, and follow God's Son. When we do these things, we inevitably partake in the spiritual abundance that the Creator has promised to those who walk in the light. But if we listen to God's instructions on Sunday morning but ignore them the rest of the week, we'll pay a heavy price for our misplaced priorities.

Every new day presents fresh opportunities to ensure that your actions are consistent with your beliefs. As a Christian leader, you owe it to yourself and your coworkers to seize those opportunities. Now.

What I believe about God
is the most important thing about me.
A. W. TOZER

GOD'S PROMISES
ABOUT BELIEFS

*Jesus said, "Because you have seen Me, you have
believed. Those who believe without seeing are blessed."*
JOHN 20:29 HCSB

*I tell you the truth, whoever believes in me
will do the same things that I do.
Those who believe will do even greater things
than these, because I am going to the Father.*
JOHN 14:12 NCV

*Most assuredly, I say to you, he who believes in Me,
the works that I do he will do also.*
JOHN 14:12 NKJV

All things are possible for the one who believes.
MARK 9:23 NCV

*I know the One I have believed in and am persuaded
that He is able to guard what has been
entrusted to me until that day.*
2 TIMOTHY 1:12 HCSB

12

BLESSINGS

May Yahweh bless you and protect you;
may Yahweh make His face shine on you
and be gracious to you;
NUMBERS 6:24-25 HCSB

Each of us has much to be thankful for. We all have more blessings than we can count, beginning with the precious gift of life. Every good gift comes from our Father above, and we owe Him our never-ending thanks. But sometimes, when the demands of everyday life press down upon us, we neglect to express our gratitude to the Creator.

God loves us and He cares for us; He has a plan for each of us; and He has offered us the gift of eternal life through His Son. Considering all the things that the Lord has done, we owe it to Him—and to ourselves—to slow down many times each day and offer our thanks. His grace is everlasting; our thanks should be, too.

God loves you and wants you to experience peace
and life—abundant and eternal.
BILLY GRAHAM

GOD'S PROMISES
ABOUT BLESSINGS

You will show me the path of life;
in Your presence is fullness of joy;
at Your right hand are pleasures forevermore.
PSALM 16:11 NKJV

The LORD is good to all:
and his tender mercies are over all his works.
PSALM 145:9 KJV

The LORD is my rock, my fortress, and my deliverer,
my God, my mountain where I seek refuge.
My shield, the horn of my salvation,
my stronghold, my refuge, and my Savior.
2 SAMUEL 22:2–3 HCSB

The LORD is my shepherd; I shall not want.
PSALM 23:1 KJV

Blessings crown the head of the righteous....
PROVERBS 10:6 NIV

13

CHANGE

To every thing there is a season,
and a time to every purpose under the heaven.
ECCLESIASTES 3:1 KJV

Here in the twenty-first century, change is a fact of life. The world keeps changing and so do we. The question, of course, is whether the changes that *we* initiate turn out to be improvements or impediments. To find the answer to that question, we must first consult a source of wisdom that does not change. That source is God.

God's Word makes it clear: "I am the LORD, I do not change" (Malachi 3:6 NKJV). We can be comforted by the knowledge that our covenant with the Creator is everlasting and nonnegotiable. The Lord has promised to keep His word, and that's precisely what He will do.

So, the next time you face tough times or unwelcome changes, remember that one thing never changes: God's love for you. Then, perhaps, you'll worry less, do your best, and leave the rest up to Him.

To improve is to change; to succeed is to change often.
WINSTON CHURCHILL

GOD'S PROMISES
ABOUT CHANGE

The wise see danger ahead and avoid it,
but fools keep going and get into trouble.
PROVERBS 22:3 NCV

But grow in the grace and knowledge of our Lord
and Savior Jesus Christ. To Him be the glory
both now and forever. Amen.
2 PETER 3:18 NKJV

When I was a child, I spoke like a child,
I thought like a child, I reasoned like a child.
When I became a man, I put aside childish things.
1 CORINTHIANS 13:11 HCSB

Then He who sat on the throne said,
"Behold, I make all things new."
REVELATION 21:5 NKJV

I am the LORD, and I do not change.
MALACHI 3:6 NLT

14

CHARACTER, HONESTY, AND INTEGRITY

Whoever walks in integrity walks securely,
but whoever takes crooked paths will be found out.
PROVERBS 10:9 NIV

Christian leaders know that integrity matters. Honesty enriches relationships and builds organizations; deception destroys them.

Henry Blackaby observed, "God is interested in developing your character. At times He lets you proceed, but He will never let you go too far without discipline to bring you back." The implication is clear: personal integrity is important to God, so it must be important to us.

Living a life of integrity isn't the easiest way, but it's always the best way. So if you find yourself tempted to break the truth—or to bend it—remember that honesty is, indeed, the best policy. It's also God's policy, so it must be your policy, too.

Character is both developed and revealed by tests,
and all of life is a test.
RICK WARREN

GOD'S PROMISES ABOUT CHARACTER, HONESTY, AND INTEGRITY

The integrity of the upright guides them,
but the perversity of the treacherous destroys them.
PROVERBS 11:3 HCSB

The godly are directed by honesty.
PROVERBS 11:5 NLT

He stores up success for the upright;
He is a shield for those who live with integrity.
PROVERBS 2:7 HCSB

The godly walk with integrity;
blessed are their children who follow them.
PROVERBS 20:7 NLT

Let integrity and uprightness preserve me,
for I wait for You.
PSALM 25:21 NKJV

15

CHARITY AND GENEROSITY

Freely you have received; freely give.
MATTHEW 10:8 NIV

The theme of generosity is woven into the fabric of God's Word. Our Creator instructs us to give generously—and cheerfully—to those in need. And He promises that when we do give of our time, our talents, and our resources, we will be blessed.

Jesus was the perfect example of generosity. He gave us everything, even His earthly life, so that we, His followers, might receive abundance, peace, and eternal life. He was always generous, always kind, always willing to help "the least of these." And, if we are to follow in His footsteps, we, too, must be generous.

Sometime today you'll encounter someone who needs a helping hand or a word of encouragement. When you encounter a person in need, think of yourself as Christ's ambassador. And remember that whatever you do for the least of these, you also do for Him.

The world asks, "What does a man own?"
Christ asks, "How does he use it?"
ANDREW MURRAY

GOD'S PROMISES ABOUT CHARITY AND GENEROSITY

So let each one give as he purposes in his heart,
not grudgingly or of necessity;
for God loves a cheerful giver.
2 CORINTHIANS 9:7 NKJV

You should remember the words of the Lord Jesus:
"It is more blessed to give than to receive."
ACTS 20:35 NLT

If you have two shirts, give one to the poor.
If you have food, share it with those who are hungry.
LUKE 3:11 NLT

Whenever we have the opportunity,
we should do good to everyone—
especially to those in the family of faith.
GALATIANS 6:10 NLT

Truly I tell you, whatever you did for one of the least
of these brothers and sisters of mine, you did for me.
MATTHEW 25:40 NIV

16

CHURCH

I was glad when they said unto me,
Let us go into the house of the LORD.
PSALM 122:1 KJV

Every church needs leaders, Christian men and women who understand the importance of sustaining—and being sustained by—their local congregations. In the book of Acts, Luke instructs us to "feed the church of God" (20:28). As Christians who have been given so much by our loving heavenly Father, we should worship Him not only in our hearts but also in the presence of fellow believers.

Today, like every other day, is a wonderful day to honor God by supporting His church. The needs are great; the laborers are few; the time for action is now; and, the blessings are real.

Every believer is commanded
to be plugged in to a local church.
DAVID JEREMIAH

GOD'S PROMISES
ABOUT CHURCH

Be on guard for yourselves and for all the flock
that the Holy Spirit has appointed you to
as overseers, to shepherd the church of God,
which He purchased with His own blood.
ACTS 20:28 HCSB

For where two or three gather in my name,
there am I with them.
MATTHEW 18:20 NIV

Enter his gates with thanksgiving;
go into his courts with praise.
Give thanks to him and praise his name.
PSALM 100:4 NLT

God is Spirit, and those who worship Him
must worship in spirit and truth.
JOHN 4:24 HCSB

Worship the Lord your God, and serve only Him.
MATTHEW 4:10 HCSB

17

CIRCUMSTANCES

Trust in him at all times, O people; pour out your hearts to him, for God is our refuge.

PSALM 62:8 NIV

From time to time, all of us must endure unpleasant circumstances. We find ourselves in situations that we didn't ask for and probably don't deserve. During these times, we try our best to "hold up under the circumstances." But God has a better plan. He intends for us to rise above our circumstances, and He's promised to help us do it.

Are you a leader who's dealing with a difficult situation or a tough problem? Do you struggle with occasional periods of discouragement and doubt? Are you worried, weary, or downcast? If so, don't face tough times alone. Face them with God as your partner, your protector, and your guide. When you do, He will give you the strength to meet any challenge, the courage to face any problem, and the patience to endure any circumstance.

God has a purpose behind every problem.
He uses circumstances to develop our character.

RICK WARREN

GOD'S PROMISES
ABOUT CIRCUMSTANCES

*The LORD is a refuge for His people
and a stronghold.*
JOEL 3:16 NASB

*The LORD is a refuge for the oppressed,
a refuge in times of trouble.*
PSALM 9:9 HCSB

*Cast your burden on the LORD,
and He shall sustain you;
He shall never permit the righteous to be moved.*
PSALM 55:22 NKJV

*God is our protection and our strength.
He always helps in times of trouble.*
PSALM 46:1 NCV

*I have learned in whatever state I am,
to be content.*
PHILIPPIANS 4:11 NKJV

18

COMMUNICATION

A word fitly spoken is like
apples of gold in settings of silver.
PROVERBS 25:11 NKJV

More often than not, great leaders are also great communicators. They understand their audience; they understand the message they want to convey; and they understand how best to convey it.

Christian leaders are bound not only by the principles of good leadership but also, more importantly, by the principles found in God's holy Word. So great Christian communicators should convey their messages with humility, with integrity, and with love.

Edwin Louis Cole had simple yet profound advice for Christian leaders in every walk of life. He said, "The truth must be spoken with love." So if you want to be an effective leader, you must learn how to be truthful without being cruel. You have the power to lift your coworkers up or to hold them back. When you learn how to lift them up, truthfully and compassionately, you'll lift yourself up, too.

Make it clear. Make it simple. Emphasize the essentials.
Forget about impressing. Leave some things unsaid.
Let the thing be simplified.
CHARLES SWINDOLL

GOD'S PROMISES
ABOUT COMMUNICATION

The heart of the wise teaches his mouth,
and adds learning to his lips.
PROVERBS 16:23 NKJV

Pleasant words are a honeycomb:
sweet to the taste and health to the body.
PROVERBS 16:24 HCSB

If anyone thinks he is religious
without controlling his tongue, then his religion
is useless and he deceives himself.
JAMES 1:26 HCSB

What you have said in the dark will be heard
in the light, and what you have whispered in
an inner room will be shouted from the housetops.
LUKE 12:3 NCV

But encourage each other daily,
while it is still called today, so that none of you
is hardened by sin's deception.
HEBREWS 3:13 HCSB

19

CONFIDENCE

So we may boldly say: "The LORD is my helper;
I will not fear. What can man do to me?"
HEBREWS 13:6 NKJV

As a leader, you need to display confidence: confidence in yourself, confidence in your plan, confidence in your team. And, as a Christian, you have every reason to live confidently. After all, you've read God's promises and you know that He's prepared a place for you in heaven. And with God on your side, what should you fear? The answer, of course, is nothing. But sometimes, despite your faith and despite God's promises, you find yourself gripped by earthly apprehensions.

When we focus on our doubts and fears, we can concoct a lengthy list of reasons to lie awake at night and fret about the uncertainties of the coming day. A better strategy, of course, is to focus, not upon our fears, but upon our God.

Are you a confident Christian? You should be. God's promises never fail and His love is everlasting. So the next time you need a boost of confidence, slow down and have a little chat with your Creator. Count your blessings, not your troubles. Focus on possibilities, not problems. And remember that with God on your side, you have absolutely nothing to fear.

He who has confidence in himself will lead the rest.
HORACE BUSHNELL

GOD'S PROMISES ABOUT CONFIDENCE

You are my hope; O Lord GOD,
You are my confidence.
PSALM 71:5 NASB

I lift up my eyes to the mountains—
where does my help come from?
My help comes from the LORD,
the Maker of heaven and earth.
PSALM 121:1-2 NIV

God is our refuge and strength,
a very present help in trouble.
PSALM 46:1 NKJV

Be strong and courageous, and do the work.
Don't be afraid or discouraged, for the LORD God,
my God, is with you. He won't leave you or forsake you.
1 CHRONICLES 28:20 HCSB

In this world you will have trouble.
But take heart! I have overcome the world.
JOHN 16:33 NIV

20

CONSCIENCE

*Now the goal of our instruction is love that comes from
a pure heart, a good conscience, and a sincere faith.*
1 TIMOTHY 1:5 HCSB

God has given each of us a conscience, and He
intends for us to use it. But sometimes we don't.
Instead of listening to that quiet inner voice that
warns us against disobedience and danger, we're
tempted to rush headlong into situations that we
soon come to regret.

God promises that He rewards good conduct and
that He blesses those who obey His Word. The Lord
also issues a stern warning to those who rebel against
His commandments. Wise leaders heed that warning.
Count yourself among their number.

Sometime soon, perhaps today, your conscience
will speak; when it does, listen carefully. God may be
trying to get a message through to you. Don't miss it.

Conscience is God's voice to the inner man.
BILLY GRAHAM

GOD'S PROMISES
ABOUT CONSCIENCE

So I strive always to keep my conscience clear
before God and man.
ACTS 24:16 NIV

Let us come near to God with a sincere heart
and a sure faith, because we have been
made free from a guilty conscience,
and our bodies have been washed with pure water.
HEBREWS 10:22 NCV

People's thoughts can be like a deep well,
but someone with understanding
can find the wisdom there.
PROVERBS 20:5 NCV

Create in me a clean heart, O God;
and renew a right spirit within me.
PSALM 51:10 KJV

Behold, the kingdom of God is within you.
LUKE 17:21 KJV

21

COOPERATION
AND TEAMWORK

*You're blessed when you can show people
how to cooperate instead of compete or fight.
That's when you discover who you really are,
and your place in God's family.*
MATTHEW 5:9 MSG

Savvy leaders understand the value of teamwork. They know that when teammates or coworkers learn the art of cooperation, everybody wins, but when cooperation breaks down, almost everybody in the organization suffers.

Are you a leader who emphasizes the importance of teamwork? Hopefully so, because in the world of sports and the world of business, cooperation pays and selfishness costs.

When everyone pulls in the same direction, mountains begin to move, but when it's "every man for himself," progress grinds to a halt. The happiest organizations are those in which everybody learns how to give and how to receive, with the emphasis on *give*.

*If a team is to reach its potential,
each player must be willing to subordinate
his personal goals to the good of the team.*
BUD WILKINSON

GOD'S PROMISES ABOUT COOPERATION AND TEAMWORK

Every kingdom divided against itself is headed for destruction, and a house divided against itself falls.
LUKE 11:17 HCSB

*Two people are better off than one,
for they can help each other succeed.*
ECCLESIASTES 4:9 NLT

*As iron sharpens iron,
so people can improve each other.*
PROVERBS 27:17 NCV

*You must get along with each other.
You must learn to be considerate of one another,
cultivating a life in common.*
1 CORINTHIANS 1:10 MSG

*A person standing alone can be attacked
and defeated, but two can stand back-to-back
and conquer. Three are even better,
for a triple-braided cord is not easily broken.*
ECCLESIASTES 4:12 NLT

22

COURAGE

Be strong and courageous, and do the work.
Do not be afraid or discouraged,
for the LORD God, my God, is with you.
1 CHRONICLES 28:20 NIV

Christians have every reason to live—and to lead—courageously. After all, Jesus promises us that He has overcome the world and that He has made a place for us in heaven. But what about those short-term, everyday worries that keep us up at night? And what about the life-altering hardships that leave us wondering if we can ever recover? The answer, of course, is that because God cares for us in good times and hard times, we can turn our concerns over to Him in prayer, knowing that all things ultimately work for the good of those who love Him.

When you form a one-on-one relationship with your Creator, you can be comforted by the fact that wherever you find yourself, whether at the top of the mountain or the depths of the valley, God is there with you. And because your Creator cares for you and protects you, you can rise above your fears.

At this very moment the Lord is seeking to work in you and through you. He's asking you to live abundantly and courageously, and He's ready to help. So why not let Him do it, starting now?

Courage is not simply one of the virtues,
but the form of every virtue at the testing point.
C. S. LEWIS

GOD'S PROMISES
ABOUT COURAGE

Be on guard. Stand firm in the faith.
Be courageous. Be strong.
1 CORINTHIANS 16:13 NLT

For God has not given us a spirit of fearfulness,
but one of power, love, and sound judgment.
2 TIMOTHY 1:7 HCSB

I can do all things through Him
who strengthens me.
PHILIPPIANS 4:13 NASB

But He said to them, "It is I;
do not be afraid."
JOHN 6:20 NKJV

Behold, God is my salvation;
I will trust, and not be afraid.
ISAIAH 12:2 KJV

23

CRITICISM

Do not judge others, and you will not be judged.
Do not condemn others, or it will all come back
against you. Forgive others, and you will be forgiven.
LUKE 6:37 NLT

Criticism comes in two flavors: constructive and destructive. Savvy leaders know the difference. They understand that a leader's role is to motivate, to encourage, to guide, and to set the right tone for the organization. The very best leaders understand that negativity breeds more negativity, so they find ways to deliver honest feedback without destroying their teammates' confidence.

You inhabit a world that's overflowing with negative messages, a world that at times seems dominated by pessimism, cynicism, doom, gloom, and very little else. Amid the sea of negativity and strife, it's easy to criticize, to complain, to moan, to groan, and to do very little else. But as a leader, you need a more constructive strategy.

So, the next time you're tempted to criticize or complain, ask yourself what you'd say if Jesus were looking over your shoulder. Because He is.

Sandwich every bit of criticism
between two heavy layers of praise.
MARY KAY ASH

GOD'S PROMISES
ABOUT CRITICISM

Whoever derides their neighbor has no sense,
but the one who has understanding holds their tongue.
PROVERBS 11:12 NIV

Do everything without grumbling and arguing,
so that you may be blameless and pure.
PHILIPPIANS 2:14–15 HCSB

Those who guard their lips preserve their lives,
but those who speak rashly will come to ruin.
PROVERBS 13:3 NIV

LORD, set up a guard for my mouth;
keep watch at the door of my lips.
PSALM 141:3 HCSB

May these words of my mouth and this meditation
of my heart be pleasing in your sight,
LORD, my Rock and my Redeemer.
PSALM 19:14 NIV

24

DECISIONS

*But if any of you needs wisdom, you should
ask God for it. He is generous to everyone
and will give you wisdom without criticizing you.*
JAMES 1:5 NCV

Leaders must make decisions, and the quality of those decisions will determine the success or failure of the endeavor. Good leaders make good decisions. Poor leaders make bad decisions. And great leaders make great decisions.

The Bible offers clear guidance about decision making. So if you're about to make an important decision, here are some things you can do:

> 1. Gather information. Don't expect to get all the facts—that's impossible—but try to gather as much information as you can in a reasonable amount of time (Proverbs 24:3–4).

> 2. Be patient. If you have time to make a decision, use that time to make a good decision (Proverbs 19:2).

> 3. Rely on the counsel of a few friends and mentors. Proverbs 1:5 makes it clear: "A wise man will hear and increase learning, and a man of understanding will attain wise counsel" (NKJV).

4. Pray for guidance and listen carefully to your conscience.

5. When the time for action arrives, act. Procrastination is the enemy of progress; don't let it defeat you (James 1:22).

You need to make the right decision—firmly and decisively—and then stick with it, with God's help.
BILLY GRAHAM

GOD'S PROMISES ABOUT DECISIONS

In every way be an example of doing good deeds. When you teach, do it with honesty and seriousness.
TITUS 2:7 NCV

We can make our own plans, but the LORD gives the right answer. People may be pure in their own eyes, but the LORD examines their motives.
PROVERBS 16:1–2 NLT

Blessed is the man who walks not in the counsel of the ungodly, nor stands in the path of sinners, nor sits in the seat of the scornful.
PSALM 1:1 NKJV

The highway of the upright avoids evil; the one who guards his way protects his life.
PROVERBS 16:17 HCSB

25

DEVOTIONALS AND QUIET TIME

Morning by morning he wakens me and opens my understanding to his will. The Sovereign LORD has spoken to me, and I have listened.

ISAIAH 50:4–5 NLT

Even the wisest leaders can't be successful by themselves. Then need mentors; they need advisors; but most of all, they need God. And if they want to maximize their leadership skills, they'll begin their day with the ultimate Counselor: their Father in heaven.

Every day of your life has 1,440 minutes, and God deserves a few of them. And you deserve the experience of spending a few quiet minutes every morning with your Creator. So, if you haven't already done so, establish the habit of spending time with God every day of the week. It's a habit that will change your day and revolutionize your life. When you give the Lord your undivided attention, everything changes, including you.

Make the Bible part of your daily life, and ask God to engrave its truths on your soul.

BILLY GRAHAM

GOD'S PROMISES ABOUT
DEVOTIONALS AND QUIET TIME

It is good to give thanks to the LORD,
and to sing praises to Your name, O Most High.
PSALM 92:1 NKJV

Heaven and earth will pass away,
but My words will never pass away.
MATTHEW 24:35 HCSB

Thy word is a lamp unto my feet,
and a light unto my path.
PSALM 119:105 KJV

Early the next morning, while it was still dark,
Jesus woke and left the house.
He went to a lonely place, where he prayed.
MARK 1:35 NCV

But grow in the grace and knowledge
of our Lord and Savior Jesus Christ. To Him be
the glory both now and to the day of eternity.
2 PETER 3:18 HCSB

26

DISCIPLINE

Discipline yourself for the purpose of godliness.
1 TIMOTHY 4:7 NASB

The best leaders understand the importance of discipline: for their followers *and* for themselves. It's not enough to preach the fine art of discipline; we must also live disciplined lives. Otherwise, our actions speak so loudly that our words become meaningless.

God does not reward apathy, laziness, or idleness, nor does He reward undisciplined behavior. Our heavenly Father has a way of helping those who first help themselves, and He expects us to lead disciplined lives despite worldly temptations to do otherwise.

The media glorifies leisure. The ultimate goal, so the message goes, is to win the lottery and then retire to some sunny paradise in order to while away the hours sitting idly by watching the waves splash onto the sand. Such leisure activities are fine for a few days, but not for a lifetime.

Life's greatest rewards are seldom the result of luck. More often than not, our greatest accomplishments require plenty of preparation and lots of work, which is perfectly fine with God. After all, He knows that we can do the work, and He knows the rewards that we'll earn when we finish the job. Besides, God

knows that He will always help us complete the tasks
He has set before us. As a matter of fact, God usually
does at least half the work: the *second* half.

*Personal discipline is a most powerful character quality
and one worthy of dedicating your life to nurturing.*
ELIZABETH GEORGE

GOD'S PROMISES
ABOUT DISCIPLINE

*Whatever you do, do your work heartily,
as for the Lord rather than for men.*
COLOSSIANS 3:23 NASB

*Better to be patient than powerful;
better to have self-control than to conquer a city.*
PROVERBS 16:32 NLT

*But the fruit of the Spirit is love, joy, peace, patience,
kindness, goodness, faith, gentleness, self-control.
Against such things there is no law.*
GALATIANS 5:22–23 HCSB

*Finishing is better than starting.
Patience is better than pride.*
ECCLESIASTES 7:8 NLT

*A final word: Be strong in the Lord
and in his mighty power.*
EPHESIANS 6:10 NLT

27

DREAMS

When dreams come true, there is life and joy.
PROVERBS 13:12 NLT

How big are your dreams? Are you expecting God to help you move mountains, or have you succumbed to pessimism and doubt? The answer to these questions will, to a surprising extent, determine the quality of your day and the direction of your life.

God has big plans for you, and He has equipped you with everything you need to make His plans come true. When the dream in your heart is one that God has placed there, miracles happen. Your challenge, of course, is to make certain that God's plans and your dreams coincide.

So keep believing in yourself, keep talking to your Creator, and keep working. And don't be afraid to dream big. After all, with God as your partner, there's no limit to the things that the two of you, working together, can accomplish.

If you can dream it, then you can achieve it.
You will get all you want in life if you help
enough other people get what they want.
ZIG ZIGLAR

GOD'S PROMISES
ABOUT DREAMS

Hope deferred makes the heart sick.
PROVERBS 13:12 NKJV

Where there is no vision, the people perish.
PROVERBS 29:18 KJV

*But we are hoping for something we do not have yet,
and we are waiting for it patiently.*
ROMANS 8:25 NCV

*Now may the God of hope fill you with all joy
and peace as you believe in him, so that you may
overflow with hope by the power of the Holy Spirit.*
ROMANS 15:13 HCSB

*Humble yourselves therefore under the mighty hand
of God, that he may exalt you in due time.*
1 PETER 5:6 KJV

28

ENCOURAGEMENT

But encourage each other daily,
while it is still called today, so that none of you
is hardened by sin's deception.
HEBREWS 3:13 HCSB

As a Christian leader, you have every reason to be hopeful, enthusiastic, and optimistic. And you have every reason to share your positive expectations with others. When you do, you'll discover that optimism, like other human emotions, is contagious.

As a follower of the One from Galilee, you have the opportunity to become a beacon of encouragement to the world. How can you do it? By looking for the good in others and celebrating the good that you find. As the old saying goes, "When someone does something good, applaud. You'll make two people happy!"

Even a brief word of appreciation can make a big difference in someone's life. So how many people will you encourage today? Ten? Twenty? Even more than that? The answer you give will help determine the quality of *their* lives *and* the quality of *yours*.

When we are the comfort and encouragement
to others, we are sometimes surprised
at how it comes back to us many times over.
BILLY GRAHAM

GOD'S PROMISES
ABOUT ENCOURAGEMENT

Let us think about each other and help
each other to show love and do good deeds.
HEBREWS 10:24 ICB

Bear one another's burdens,
and so fulfill the law of Christ.
GALATIANS 6:2 NKJV

So encourage each other and give each other strength,
just as you are doing now.
1 THESSALONIANS 5:11 NCV

When you talk, do not say harmful things,
but say what people need—words that will help
others become stronger. Then what you say
will do good to those who listen to you.
EPHESIANS 4:29 NCV

Now we exhort you, brethren,
warn those who are unruly,
comfort the fainthearted,
uphold the weak, be patient with all.
1 THESSALONIANS 5:14 NKJV

29

ENTHUSIASM

Whatever you do, do it enthusiastically,
as something done for the Lord and not for men.
COLOSSIANS 3:23 HCSB

As a Christian leader, you have many reasons to be enthusiastic about your life, your opportunities, your team, and your future. After all, your eternal destiny is secure. Christ died for your sins, and He wants you to experience life abundant and life eternal. So what's not to get excited about?

Are you an enthusiastic leader and a passionate Christian? Are you genuinely excited about your faith, your career, and your future? Hopefully you can answer these questions with a resounding yes. But if your passion for the tasks of life has waned, it's time to slow down long enough to recharge your spiritual batteries, reflect on your plans, and then reorder your priorities.

Each new day is an opportunity to put God first and celebrate His creation. Today, take time to count your blessings and take stock of your opportunities. And while you're at it, ask God for strength. When you sincerely petition Him, He will give you everything you need to live well and lead well.

Wherever you are, be all there. Live to the hilt every
situation you believe to be the will of God.
JIM ELLIOT

GOD'S PROMISES
ABOUT ENTHUSIASM

Do your work with enthusiasm.
Work as if you were serving the Lord,
not as if you were serving only men and women.
EPHESIANS 6:7 NCV

A happy heart makes the face cheerful,
but heartache crushes the spirit.
PROVERBS 15:13 NIV

But as for me, I will hope continually,
and will praise You yet more and more.
PSALM 71:14 NASB

Rejoice always! Pray constantly.
Give thanks in everything, for this is God's will
for you in Christ Jesus.
1 THESSALONIANS 5:16–18 HCSB

Let the hearts of those who seek the LORD rejoice.
Look to the LORD and his strength; seek his face always.
1 CHRONICLES 16:10–11 NIV

30

EXAMPLE

*You should be an example to the believers in speech,
in conduct, in love, in faith, in purity.*
1 TIMOTHY 4:12 HCSB

All of us are role models. Whether we like it or not, our actions speak volumes—much more loudly, in fact, than our words—to friends, to family members, to coworkers, and to teammates What kind of example are you? Are your actions encouraging others to follow in the footsteps of God's Son? Hopefully so.

You live in a dangerous, distraction-filled world, brimming with temptations. That's why you encounter so many opportunities to stray from God's path. Your task, of course, is to avoid the distractions and reject the temptations. When you do, you'll serve as a powerful example and a positive role model in a world that desperately needs both.

Our walk counts far more than our talk, always!
GEORGE MUELLER

GOD'S PROMISES
ABOUT BEING AN EXAMPLE

*For you were once darkness, but now you are light
in the Lord. Walk as children of light—for the fruit
of the light results in all goodness, righteousness,
and truth—discerning what is pleasing to the Lord.*
EPHESIANS 5:8–10 HCSB

If we live in the Spirit, let us also walk in the Spirit.
GALATIANS 5:25 NKJV

*Who among you is wise and understanding?
Let him show by his good behavior
his deeds in the gentleness of wisdom.*
JAMES 3:13 NASB

*But prove yourselves doers of the word,
and not merely hearers who delude themselves.*
JAMES 1:22 NASB

*In any case, we should live up to whatever
truth we have attained.*
PHILIPPIANS 3:16 HCSB

31

EXCELLENCE

Whatever you do, work at it with all your heart,
as working for the Lord, not for human masters.
COLOSSIANS 3:23 NIV

The legendary football coach Vince Lombardi observed, "The quality of a person's life is in direct proportion to his commitment to excellence, regardless of his chosen field of endeavor." Wise leaders agree. The rewards of excellence are many; the rewards of mediocrity are few.

The Lord has created a world in which quality work is rewarded and sloppy work is not. Yet sometimes we're tempted to seek ease over excellence. Or we may—mistakenly—search for shortcuts when God intends that we take a different, more rigorous path.

So, wherever you find yourself, whether you're leading a Fortune 500 company or building a startup business in your garage, strive for excellence. Strive for quality solutions, not quick-and-easy-fixes. When you do, your work will be rewarded and God will find a way to bless your efforts. Simply do your best, with determination and purpose, and leave the rest up to Him.

The quest for excellence is a mark of maturity.
MAX LUCADO

GOD'S PROMISES
ABOUT EXCELLENCE

Finally, brothers and sisters, whatever is true,
whatever is noble, whatever is right,
whatever is pure, whatever is lovely,
whatever is admirable—
if anything is excellent or praiseworthy—
think about such things.
PHILIPPIANS 4:8 NIV

His master replied, "Well done,
good and faithful servant!
You have been faithful with a few things;
I will put you in charge of many things.
Come and share your master's happiness!"
MATTHEW 25:21 NIV

Now the God of peace...make you perfect
in every good work to do his will,
working in you that which
is wellpleasing in his sight.
HEBREWS 13:20–21 KJV

32

FAILURE

For though the righteous fall seven times,
they rise again.
PROVERBS 24:16 NIV

Occasional mistakes, setbacks, disappointments, and failures are the price that we must pay for taking risks and trying new things. Even the best-intentioned plans sometimes go astray, and when they do, we must never lose faith. When we fail, we must not label ourselves as "failures." Instead, we should pick ourselves up, dust ourselves off, learn from our mistakes, and reengage with life.

Have you encountered a recent setback? If so, what did you learn? And how can you apply your hard-earned wisdom to the challenges that are ahead of you?

If you've experienced a recent disappointment, remember that God still has big plans for your life. And while you're waiting for those plans to unfold, keep working, keep praying, and keep the faith. The Lord can build a road through any wilderness. Even yours.

Don't be bound by the past and its failures.
But don't forgets its lessons either.
BILLY GRAHAM

GOD'S PROMISES
ABOUT FAILURE

The LORD is near to those who have a broken heart.
PSALM 34:18 NKJV

If you listen to correction to improve your life,
you will live among the wise.
PROVERBS 15:31 NCV

We are hard-pressed on every side,
yet not crushed;
we are perplexed,
but not in despair.
2 CORINTHIANS 4:8 NKJV

But as for you, be strong; don't be discouraged,
for your work has a reward.
2 CHRONICLES 15:7 HCSB

Weeping may endure for a night,
but joy cometh in the morning.
PSALM 30:5 KJV

33

FAITH

For truly I say to you, if you have faith the size
of a mustard seed, you will say to this mountain,
"Move from here to there," and it will move;
and nothing will be impossible to you.
MATTHEW 17:20 NASB

The Bible makes it clear—and Christian leaders understand—that faith is powerful. With it we can move mountains. With it we can endure any hardship. With it we can rise above the challenges of everyday life and live victoriously, whatever our circumstances.

Is your faith strong enough to move the mountains in your own life? If so, you're already tapped in to a source of strength that never fails: God's strength. But if your spiritual batteries are in need of recharging, don't be discouraged. God's strength is always available to those who seek.

The first element of a successful life is faith: faith in God, faith in His promises, and faith in His Son. When our faith in the Creator is strong, we can then have faith in ourselves, knowing that we are tools in the hands of a loving God who made mountains— and moves them—according to a perfect plan that only He can see.

Fear imprisons, faith liberates; fear paralyzes,
faith empowers; fear disheartens, faith encourages;
fear sickens, faith heals; fear makes useless,
faith makes serviceable.

HARRY EMERSON FOSDICK

GOD'S PROMISES
ABOUT FAITH

Don't be afraid, because I am your God.
I will make you strong and will help you;
I will support you with my right hand that saves you.

ISAIAH 41:10 NCV

Don't be afraid. Only believe.

MARK 5:36 HCSB

Blessed are they that have not seen,
and yet have believed.

JOHN 20:29 KJV

All things are possible for the one who believes.

MARK 9:23 NCV

And he said unto her, Daughter, thy faith hath
made thee whole; go in peace, and be whole.

MARK 5:34 KJV

34

FEAR

*Peace I leave with you; My peace I give to you;
not as the world gives do I give to you.
Do not let your heart be troubled, nor let it be fearful.*
JOHN 14:27 NASB

All leaders experience difficult days when unexpected circumstances test their mettle. Difficult times call for courageous measures. Running away from problems only perpetuates them; fear begets more fear; and anxiety is a poor counselor. As John Maxwell observed, "People who focus on their fears don't grow. They become paralyzed."

Adversity visits everyone—no human being is beyond Old Man Trouble's reach. But Old Man Trouble is more than an unwelcome guest; he is also an invaluable teacher. If we are to become mature human beings, it is our duty to learn from the inevitable hardships and disappointments of life.

Today, ask God to help you step beyond the boundaries of your fear. Ask Him to guide you to a place where you can realize your potential and help others reach theirs. Ask Him to do His part, and then promise Him that you'll do your part. Don't ask God to lead you to a safe place; ask Him to lead you to the right place. And remember that those two places are seldom the same.

The presence of fear does not mean
you have no faith. Fear visits everyone.
But make your fear a visitor and not a resident.
MAX LUCADO

GOD'S PROMISES
ABOUT FEAR

But He said to them, "It is I; do not be afraid."
JOHN 6:20 NKJV

Fear not, for I am with you; be not dismayed,
for I am your God. I will strengthen you,
yes, I will help you, I will uphold you
with My righteous right hand.
ISAIAH 41:10 NKJV

The LORD is my light and my salvation—
whom should I fear? The LORD is the stronghold
of my life—of whom should I be afraid?
PSALM 27:1 HCSB

Even though I walk through the darkest valley ,
I will fear no evil, for you are with me;
your rod and your staff, they comfort me.
PSALM 23:4 NIV

Be not afraid, only believe.
MARK 5:36 KJV

35

FOLLOWING CHRIST

Then He said to them all, "If anyone wants
to come with Me, he must deny himself,
take up his cross daily, and follow Me."
LUKE 9:23 HCSB

Every day, we're presented with countless opportunities to honor God by following in the footsteps of His Son. But we're sorely tempted to do otherwise. The world is filled to the brim with temptations and distractions that beckon us down a different path.

Bill Bright observed, "We must always invite Jesus to be the navigator of our plans, desires, wills, and emotions, for He is the way, the truth, and the life."

Today, don't just be a leader. Be a follower, too: a follower of the One from Galilee. Do your part to take up the cross and follow Him, even if the world encourages you to do otherwise. When you're traveling step-by-step with the Son of God, you're always on the right path.

To be a disciple of Jesus means to learn from Him,
to follow Him. The cost may be high.
BILLY GRAHAM

GOD'S PROMISES
ABOUT FOLLOWING CHRIST

*But whoever keeps His word, truly in him
the love of God is perfected. This is how we know
we are in Him: the one who says he remains
in Him should walk just as He walked.*
1 John 2:5–6 HCSB

*Walk in a manner worthy of the God who calls you
into His own kingdom and glory.*
1 Thessalonians 2:12 NASB

For we walk by faith, not by sight.
2 Corinthians 5:7 HCSB

*Take my yoke upon you, and learn of me;
for I am meek and lowly in heart: and ye shall
find rest unto your souls. For my yoke is easy,
and my burden is light.*
Matthew 11:29–30 KJV

*Whoever is not willing to carry the cross and follow
me is not worthy of me. Those who try to hold on
to their lives will give up true life. Those who
give up their lives for me will hold on to true life.*
Matthew 10:38–39 NCV

36

FORGIVENESS

Judge not, and you shall not be judged.
Condemn not, and you shall not be condemned.
Forgive, and you will be forgiven.
LUKE 6:37 NKJV

Forgiveness is a gift of great value, but ironically it's a gift that is often worth more to the giver than to the recipient. You simply cannot give the gift of forgiveness without receiving an important blessing for yourself.

From a psychological perspective, the act of forgiving relieves you of some very heavy mental baggage: persistent feelings of hatred, anger, and regret. More importantly, the act of forgiveness brings with it a spiritual blessing, a knowledge that you have honored your heavenly Father by obeying His commandments.

Simply put, forgiveness is a gift that you give yourself by giving it to someone else. When you make the choice to forgive, everybody wins, including you.

Forgiveness is one of the most beautiful words
in the human vocabulary. How much pain could
be avoided if we all learned the meaning of this word!
BILLY GRAHAM

GOD'S PROMISES
ABOUT FORGIVENESS

Above all, love each other deeply,
because love covers over a multitude of sins.
1 PETER 4:8 NIV

But I say to you, love your enemies,
and pray for those who persecute you.
MATTHEW 5:44 NASB

And be kind to one another,
tenderhearted, forgiving one another,
just as God in Christ forgave you.
EPHESIANS 4:32 NKJV

And whenever you stand praying,
if you have anything against anyone,
forgive him, so that your Father in heaven
may also forgive you your wrongdoing.
MARK 11:25 HCSB

The merciful are blessed,
for they will be shown mercy.
MATTHEW 5:7 HCSB

37

GIFTS

Do not neglect the gift that is in you.
1 TIMOTHY 4:14 NKJV

God gives each of us special talents and opportunities. And He bestows these gifts for a reason: so that we might use them for His glory. But the world tempts us to do otherwise. Here in the twenty-first century, life is filled to the brim with distractions and temptations, each of which has the potential to distance us from the path God intends for us to take.

Do you possess financial resources? Share them. Do you have a spiritual gift? Share it. Do you have a personal testimony about the things that Christ has done for you? Tell your story. Do you possess a particular talent? Hone that skill and use it for God's glory.

All your talents, all your opportunities, and all your gifts are on temporary loan from the Creator. Use those gifts while you can because time is short and the needs are great. In every undertaking, make God your partner. Then, just as He promised, God will bless you now and forever.

You weren't an accident. You weren't mass produced. You aren't an assembly-line product. You were deliberately planned, specifically gifted, and lovingly positioned on the earth by the Master Craftsman.
MAX LUCADO

GOD'S PROMISES
ABOUT HIS GIFTS

God has given each of you a gift
from his great variety of spiritual gifts.
Use them well to serve one another.
1 PETER 4:10 NLT

Now there are diversities of gifts, but the same Spirit.
1 CORINTHIANS 12:4 KJV

Every good and perfect gift is from above,
coming down from the Father of the heavenly lights,
who does not change like shifting shadows.
JAMES 1:17 NIV

His master replied, "Well done, good and faithful
servant! You have been faithful with a few things;
I will put you in charge of many things.
Come and share your master's happiness!"
MATTHEW 25:21 NIV

I remind you to fan into flame the gift of God.
2 TIMOTHY 1:6 NIV

38

GOD FIRST

You shall have no other gods before Me.
EXODUS 20:3 NKJV

Wise leaders understand the importance of doing first things first. And wise Christians understand the importance of putting God first in every aspect of life, including the workplace.

If you're a Christian leader, these are very busy times. You have so many obligations and so little time. From the moment you rise until you drift off to sleep at night, you have things to do, meetings to attend, and people to contact. So how do you find time for God? You must make time for Him, plain and simple. When you put God first, you're blessed. But if you succumb to the pressures and temptations of the world, you'll inevitably pay a price.

In the book of Exodus, God warns that we should put no gods before Him. Yet all too often we place our Lord in second, third, or fourth place as we focus on other things. When we place our desires for possessions and status above our love for God, or when we yield to the countless distractions that surround us, we forfeit the peace that might otherwise be ours.

In the wilderness, Satan offered Jesus earthly power and unimaginable riches, but Jesus refused. Instead, He chose to worship His heavenly Father.

We must do likewise by putting God first and worshiping Him only. God must come first. Always first.

Jesus Christ is the first and last, author and finisher, beginning and end, alpha and omega, and by Him all other things hold together. He must be first or nothing. God never comes next!

VANCE HAVNER

GOD'S PROMISES ABOUT PUTTING HIM FIRST

In everything you do, put God first, and he will direct you and crown your efforts with success.
PROVERBS 3:6 TLB

My choice is you, God, first and only.
PSALM 16:5 MSG

Take your everyday, ordinary life—your sleeping, eating, going-to-work, and walking-around life—and place it before God as an offering. Embracing what God does for you is the best thing you can do for him.
ROMANS 12:1 MSG

39

GOD'S CALLING

*I urge you to live a life worthy of
the calling you have received.*
EPHESIANS 4:1 NIV

God created you on purpose. He has a plan for
your life that only you, as a Christian leader—
with your own unique array of talents and your own
particular set of circumstances—can fulfill. The Lord
is gently guiding you to the place where you can
accomplish the greatest good for yourself and for His
kingdom.

Have you already heard God's call? And are you
doing your best to pursue His plan for your life? If
so, you're blessed. But if you have not yet discovered
God's plan for your life, don't panic. There's still time
to hear His call and follow His path. To find that
path, keep searching and keep praying. Answers
will come.

The Creator has placed you in a particular
location, amid particular people, with particular
responsibilities, and with unique opportunities to
serve. And He has given you all the tools you need to
accomplish His plans. So listen for His voice, watch
for His signs, and prepare yourself for the call—
His call—that is certain to come.

There's some task which the God of all the universe,
the great Creator, has for you to do, and which
will remain undone and incomplete until by faith and
obedience, you step into the will of God.
ALAN REDPATH

GOD'S PROMISES
ABOUT HIS CALLING

But as God has distributed to each one,
as the Lord has called each one, so let him walk.
1 CORINTHIANS 7:17 NKJV

And we know that all things work together
for good to those who love God, to those who are
the called according to His purpose.
ROMANS 8:28 NKJV

For whoever does the will of God is My brother
and My sister and mother.
MARK 3:35 NKJV

For many are called, but few are chosen.
MATTHEW 22:14 KJV

For you have need of endurance,
so that when you have done the will of God,
you may receive what was promised.
HEBREWS 10:36 NASB

40

GOD'S GUIDANCE

*Trust in the LORD with all your heart, and lean not
on your own understanding; in all your ways
acknowledge Him, and He shall direct your paths.*
PROVERBS 3:5–6 NKJV

Leaders give guidance and receive it. And the best
guidance inevitably comes from God. When we
open our hearts and minds to His direction, He will
lead us along a path of His choosing. But for many
of us, listening to God is hard. We have so many
things we want, and so many needs to pray for, that
we spend far more time talking at God than we do
listening to Him.

Oswald Chambers advised, "Get into the habit
of dealing with God about everything." These words
remind us that life is best lived when we seek the
Lord's direction early and often.

Our Father has many ways to make Himself
known. Our challenge is to make ourselves open to
His instruction. So, if you're unsure of your next step,
trust God's promises and talk to Him often. When
you do, He'll guide your steps today, tomorrow, and
forever.

God is the silent partner in all great enterprises.
ABRAHAM LINCOLN

GOD'S PROMISES
ABOUT HIS GUIDANCE

Yet Lᴏʀᴅ, You are our Father; we are the clay,
and You are our potter; we all are the work of Your hands.
Isᴀɪᴀʜ 64:8 HCSB

The Lᴏʀᴅ says, "I will guide you along
the best pathway for your life. I will advise you
and watch over you."
Psᴀʟᴍ 32:8 NLT

Teach me to do Your will, for You are my God;
Your Spirit is good. Lead me in the land of uprightness.
Psᴀʟᴍ 143:10 NKJV

Shew me thy ways, O Lᴏʀᴅ; teach me thy paths.
Lead me in thy truth, and teach me: for thou art
the God of my salvation; on thee do I wait all the day.
Psᴀʟᴍ 25:4–5 KJV

Morning by morning he wakens me and opens
my understanding to his will. The Sovereign Lᴏʀᴅ
has spoken to me, and I have listened.
Isᴀɪᴀʜ 50:4–5 NLT

41

GOD'S TIMING

Therefore humble yourselves under the mighty
hand of God, that He may exalt you in due time.
1 PETER 5:6 NKJV

If you're like most people—and like most leaders—
you're in a hurry. You know precisely what you
want, and you know precisely when you want it:
as soon as possible. Because your time on earth is
limited, you may feel a sense of urgency. God does
not. There is no panic in heaven.

Our heavenly Father, in His infinite wisdom,
operates according to His own timetable, not ours.
He has plans that we cannot see and purposes that
we cannot know. He has created a world that unfolds
according to His own schedule. Thank goodness!
After all, He is omniscient; His is trustworthy; and
He knows what's best for us.

If you've been waiting impatiently for the Lord to
answer your prayers, it's time to put a stop to all that
needless worry. You can be sure that God will answer
your prayers when the time is right. You job is to keep
praying—and working—until He does.

Will not the Lord's time be better than your time?
C. H. SPURGEON

GOD'S PROMISES
ABOUT HIS TIMING

God has made everything beautiful for its own time.
ECCLESIASTES 3:11 NIV

He has made everything appropriate in its time.
He has also put eternity in their hearts,
but man cannot discover the work
God has done from beginning to end.
ECCLESIASTES 3:11 HCSB

Yet the LORD longs to be gracious to you;
therefore he will rise up to show you compassion.
For the LORD is a God of justice.
Blessed are all who wait for him!
ISAIAH 30:18 NIV

Trust in the LORD with all your heart,
and lean not on your own understanding;
in all your ways acknowledge Him,
and He shall direct your paths.
PROVERBS 3:5–6 NKJV

To every thing there is a season,
and a time to every purpose under the heaven.
ECCLESIASTES 3:1 KJV

42

HELPING OTHERS

Carry one another's burdens; in this way
you will fulfill the law of Christ.
GALATIANS 6:2 HCSB

Servant-leaders are in the business of helping others. And if you're looking for somebody to help, you won't have to look very far. Somebody nearby needs a helping hand, or a hot meal, or a pat on the back, or a prayer. In order to find that person, you'll need to keep your eyes and your heart open, and you'll need to stay focused on the needs of others. Focusing, however, is not as simple as it seems.

We live in a fast-paced, media-driven world filled with countless temptations and time-wasting distractions. Sometimes we may convince ourselves that we simply don't have the time or the resources to offer help to the needy. Such thoughts are misguided. Caring for our neighbors must be *our* priority because it is *God's* priority.

God has placed you here and given you particular responsibilities. He has a specific plan for your life, and part of that plan involves service to coworkers, teammates friends, family members, and complete strangers. Service, like leadership, is not a burden; it's an opportunity. Seize your opportunity today. Tomorrow may be too late.

A true servant of God
is one who helps another succeed.
BILLY GRAHAM

GOD'S PROMISES
ABOUT HELPING OTHERS

Let us not become weary in doing good,
for at the proper time we will reap
a harvest if we do not give up.
GALATIANS 6:9 NIV

Whenever you are able,
do good to people who need help.
PROVERBS 3:27 NCV

If you have two shirts, give one to the poor.
If you have food, share it with those who are hungry.
LUKE 3:11 NLT

Whatever you did for one of the least
of these brothers of Mine, you did for Me.
MATTHEW 25:40 HCSB

Therefore, as we have opportunity, we must
work for the good of all, especially for those
who belong to the household of faith.
GALATIANS 6:10 HCSB

43

HOPE

Let us hold fast the confession of our hope without wavering, for He who promised is faithful.
HEBREWS 10:23 NASB

God's promises give us hope: hope for today, hope for tomorrow, hope for all eternity. The hope that the world offers is temporary, at best. But the hope that God offers never grows old and never goes out of date. It's no wonder, then, that when we pin our hopes on worldly resources, we are often disappointed. Thankfully, God has no such record of failure.

The Bible teaches that the Lord blesses those who trust in His wisdom and follow in the footsteps of His Son. Will you count yourself among that number? When you do, you'll have every reason on earth—and in heaven—to be hopeful about your future. After all, God has made important promises to you, promises that He is certainly going to keep. So be hopeful, be optimistic, be faithful, and do your best. Then, leave the rest up to God. Your destiny is safe with Him.

The presence of hope in the invincible sovereignty of God drives out fear.
JOHN PIPER

GOD'S PROMISES
ABOUT HOPE

This hope we have as an anchor of the soul,
a hope both sure and steadfast.
HEBREWS 6:19 NASB

I say to myself, "The LORD is mine,
so I hope in him."
LAMENTATIONS 3:24 NCV

The LORD is good to those who wait for Him,
to the soul who seeks Him. It is good that one should
hope and wait quietly for the salvation of the LORD.
LAMENTATIONS 3:25–26 NKJV

Hope deferred makes the heart sick,
But when the desire comes, it is a tree of life.
PROVERBS 13:12 NKJV

Be strong and courageous,
all you who put your hope in the LORD.
PSALM 31:24 HCSB

44

HUMILITY

Therefore humble yourselves under the mighty hand of God, that He may exalt you in due time, casting all your care upon Him, for He cares for you.
1 PETER 5:6-7 NKJV

We humans are often tempted by a dangerous, debilitating sin: pride. Even though God's Word clearly warns us that pride is hazardous to our spiritual health, we're still tempted to brag about our accomplishments and overstate them. We're tempted to puff ourselves up by embellishing our victories and concealing our defeats. But in truth, all of us are mere mortals who have many more reasons to be humble than prideful.

As Christians who have been saved, not by our own good works but by God's grace, how can we be prideful? The answer, of course, is that if we are honest with ourselves and with our God we simply can't be boastful. We must, instead, be filled with humble appreciation for the things God has done. Our good works are minuscule compared to His. Whatever happens, the Lord deserves the credit, not us. And if we're wise, we'll give Him all the credit He deserves.

Faith itself cannot be strong where humility is weak.
C. H. SPURGEON

GOD'S PROMISES
ABOUT HUMILITY

Always be humble, gentle, and patient,
accepting each other in love.
EPHESIANS 4:2 NCV

Humble yourselves in the sight of the Lord,
and he shall lift you up.
JAMES 4:10 KJV

For everyone who exalts himself will be humbled,
and the one who humbles himself will be exalted.
LUKE 14:11 HCSB

Therefore, God's chosen ones, holy and loved,
put on heartfelt compassion, kindness,
humility, gentleness, and patience.
COLOSSIANS 3:12 HCSB

Blessed are the meek:
for they shall inherit the earth.
MATTHEW 5:5 KJV

45

JOY

This is the day which the LORD has made;
let us rejoice and be glad in it.
PSALM 118:24 NASB

The joy that the world offers is fleeting and in-complete: here today, gone tomorrow, not coming back anytime soon. But God's joy is different. His joy has staying power. In fact, it's a gift that never stops giving to those who welcome His Son into their hearts.

Psalm 100 reminds us to celebrate the lives that God has given us: "Shout for joy to the LORD, all the earth. Worship the LORD with gladness; come before Him with joyful songs." (v. 1–2 NIV). Yet sometimes amid the inevitable complications and predicaments that are woven into the fabric of everyday life, we forget to rejoice. Instead of celebrating life, we com-plain about it. This is an understandable mistake, but a mistake nonetheless. As Christians, we are called by our Creator to live joyfully and abundantly. To do otherwise is to squander His spiritual gifts.

This day and every day, Christ offers you His peace and His joy. Accept it and share it with others, just as He has shared His joy with you.

Joy is the serious business of heaven.
C. S. LEWIS

GOD'S PROMISES
ABOUT JOY

Rejoice in the Lord always.
Again I will say, rejoice!
PHILIPPIANS 4:4 NKJV

Rejoice always, pray without ceasing,
in everything give thanks; for this is the will of God
in Christ Jesus for you.
1 THESSALONIANS 5:16–18 NKJV

I have spoken these things to you so that
My joy may be in you and your joy may be complete.
JOHN 15:11 HCSB

Until now you have asked for nothing
in My name. Ask and you will receive,
so that your joy may be complete.
JOHN 16:24 HCSB

So you also have sorrow now. But I will
see you again. Your hearts will rejoice,
and no one will rob you of your joy.
JOHN 16:22 HCSB

46

KINDNESS AND COMPASSION

*Therefore, whatever you want men to do to you,
do also to them, for this is the Law and the Prophets.*
MATTHEW 7:12 NKJV

Jesus set the example: He was compassionate, loving, and kind. If we, as Christian leaders, seek to follow Him, we, too, must combine compassionate hearts with willing hands.

John Wesley said: "Do all the good you can. By all the means you can. In all the ways you can. In all the places you can. At all the times you can. To all the people you can. As long as ever you can." His advice still applies. In order to follow in Christ's footsteps, we must be compassionate. There is simply no other way.

Never underestimate the power of kindness. You never know when a kind word or gesture might significantly improve someone's day, or week, or life. So be quick to offer words of encouragement, and smiles, and pats on the back. Be generous with your resources and your time. Make kindness the cornerstone of your dealings with others. They will be blessed, and you will be, too. And everybody wins.

All around you are people whose lives
are filled with trouble and sorrow.
They need your compassion and encouragement.
BILLY GRAHAM

GOD'S PROMISES ABOUT
KINDNESS AND COMPASSION

A new commandment I give unto you,
That ye love one another; as I have loved you,
that ye also love one another.
JOHN 13:34 KJV

Who is wise and has understanding among you?
He should show his works by good conduct
with wisdom's gentleness.
JAMES 3:13 HCSB

Be kind to one another, tender-hearted, forgiving
each other, just as God in Christ also has forgiven you.
EPHESIANS 4:32 NASB

And let us not grow weary while doing good,
for in due season we shall reap if we do not lose heart.
GALATIANS 6:9 NKJV

Assuredly, I say to you, inasmuch as you did it to one
of the least of these My brethren, you did it to Me.
MATTHEW 25:40 NKJV

47

KNOWLEDGE

Wisdom is the principal thing; therefore get wisdom.
And in all your getting, get understanding.
PROVERBS 4:7 NKJV

What does it take to become wise? Experience helps. So does education. Common sense helps, and mentors help, too. But the best wisdom, and the most important, is found between the covers of the book God wrote. So, if you sincerely desire to become wise, you must begin by studying His Word. In it, you'll find everything you need to live wisely and well.

Warren Wiersbe observed, "Wise people listen to wise instruction, especially instruction from the Word of God." Savvy Christian leaders agree.

So, if you need technical knowledge, grab a textbook or take a class. And if you need more education, go back to school. But if you're searching for eternal truths—the kind of wisdom that doesn't change with the shifting tides of popular opinion—the best way to start is by opening your Bible and opening your heart to God. When you do, you'll discover that His wisdom always applies and His guidance never fails.

I am still learning, for the Christian life
is one of constant growth.
BILLY GRAHAM

GOD'S PROMISES
ABOUT KNOWLEDGE

Commit yourself to instruction;
listen carefully to words of knowledge.
PROVERBS 23:12 NLT

Enthusiasm without knowledge is not good.
If you act too quickly, you might make a mistake.
PROVERBS 19:2 NCV

Joyful is the person who finds wisdom,
the one who gains understanding.
PROVERBS 3:13 NLT

Teach me Your way, Yahweh,
and I will live by Your truth.
Give me an undivided mind to fear Your name.
PSALM 86:11 HCSB

I will show you what someone is like who comes
to Me, hears My words, and acts on them:
He is like a man building a house, who dug deep
and laid the foundation on the rock.
When the flood came, the river crashed against that
house and couldn't shake it, because it was well built.
LUKE 6:47–48 HCSB

48

LEADERSHIP

But a good leader plans to do good,
and those good things make him a good leader.
ISAIAH 32:8 NCV

The world defines leadership in many ways, oftentimes using vague platitudes and general descriptions. But God's definition is more specific. He's looking for servant-leaders who are willing to follow in the footsteps of His only begotten Son. And He's always willing to help those men and women who genuinely place His priorities first.

If you're seriously considering Christian leadership, then you must be equally serious about Christian service. After all, Jesus Himself came, not as a conquering autocrat but as a humble servant. For those who seek to follow Him—and lead others along that same path—a genuine commitment to service is not optional. It's required.

A leader is one who knows the way,
goes the way, and shows the way.
JOHN MAXWELL

GOD'S PROMISES
ABOUT LEADERSHIP

Shepherd the flock of God which is among you.
1 PETER 5:2 NKJV

An overseer, therefore, must be above reproach,
the husband of one wife, self-controlled, sensible,
respectable, hospitable, an able teacher,
not addicted to wine, not a bully but gentle,
not quarrelsome, not greedy.
1 TIMOTHY 3:2–3 HCSB

Those who are wise will shine like the brightness
of the heavens, and those who lead many
to righteousness, like the stars for ever and ever.
DANIEL 12:3 NIV

Therefore encourage one another and build up
one another, just as you also are doing.
1 THESSALONIANS 5:11 NASB

Good leaders cultivate honest speech;
they love advisors who tell them the truth.
PROVERBS 16:13 MSG

49

MENTORS

A wise man will hear and increase learning,
and a man of understanding will attain wise counsel.
PROVERBS 1:5 NKJV

The Roman playwright Plautus said, "None of us are wise enough by ourselves." What was true in 200 BC is still true today. In today's fast-changing world, we need the benefit of good counsel, informed opinions, and honest advice.

Even the wisest leaders can't be successful by themselves. They need trustworthy mentors and competent counselors. And, if you wish to become a skilled leader, you'll need advisors, too.

So, the next time you're facing a big decision, don't be too proud to ask for advice. Then, when you've sought the opinions of people you trust, consult the ultimate Counselor: your Father in heaven. With His guidance, and with the help of trusted friends and mentors, you can make important decisions with confidence.

You're never too young to be taught
and never too old to teach.
EDWIN LOUIS COLE

GOD'S PROMISES
ABOUT MENTORS

Listen to advice and accept correction,
and in the end you will be wise.
PROVERBS 19:20 NCV

How much better to get wisdom than gold,
to get insight rather than silver!
PROVERBS 16:16 NIV

Those who are wise shall shine like the brightness
of the firmament, and those who turn many
to righteousness like the stars forever and ever.
DANIEL 12:3 NKJV

Iron sharpens iron, and one man sharpens another.
PROVERBS 27:17 HCSB

A fool's way is right in his own eyes,
but whoever listens to counsel is wise.
PROVERBS 12:15 HCSB

50

MIRACLES

Is anything too hard for the LORD?
GENESIS 18:14 NKJV

God's power has no limitations. He is not restrained by the laws of nature because He created those laws. At any time, at any place, under any set of circumstances, He can accomplish anything He chooses. The things that seem miraculous to us are, to Him, expressions of His power and His love.

Do you expect God to work miracles in your own life? You should. From the moment He created our universe out of nothingness, the Lord has made a habit of doing miraculous things. And He's still working miracles today.

With God nothing is impossible. His wondrous works come in all shapes and sizes, so keep your eyes and your heart open. Somewhere, a miracle is about to happen, and it might just happen *to you.*

The same Jesus Who turned water into wine can transform your home, your life, your family, and your future. He is still in the miracle-working business, and His business is the business of transformation.
ADRIAN ROGERS

GOD'S PROMISES
ABOUT MIRACLES

*God confirmed the message by giving signs
and wonders and various miracles and gifts
of the Holy Spirit whenever he chose.*
HEBREWS 2:4 NLT

*What no eye has seen, what no ear has heard,
and what no human mind has conceived—
the things God has prepared for those who love him.*
1 CORINTHIANS 2:9 NIV

*You are the God of great wonders!
You demonstrate your awesome power
among the nations.*
PSALM 77:14 NLT

*And Jesus looking upon them saith,
With men it is impossible, but not with God:
for with God all things are possible.*
MARK 10:27 KJV

For with God nothing shall be impossible.
LUKE 1:37 KJV

51

MISTAKES

If we confess our sins to him, he is faithful and just to forgive us and to cleanse us from all wickedness.
1 JOHN 1:9 NLT

None of us are perfect; we all make mistakes. The question, then, is not *whether* we'll make mistakes but *what* we'll do about them. If we focus on covering up instead of fixing, we invite even more troubles. But if we learn from our mistakes and make amends whenever possible, God will help us make use of our setbacks.

Have you recently made a mistake that caused trouble, disappointment, or heartbreak? If so, look for the lesson that the Lord is trying to teach you. Instead of grumbling about life's sad state of affairs, learn what needs to be learned, change what needs to be changed, and move on. View every major setback as an opportunity to reassess God's will for your life. And while you're at it, consider your mistakes to be powerful opportunities to learn more about yourself, your circumstances, and your world.

Everybody (including you) makes mistakes. Your job is to make them only once. And with God's help, you can do it.

A man must be big enough to admit his mistakes,
smart enough to profit from them,
and strong enough to correct them.
JOHN MAXWELL

GOD'S PROMISES
ABOUT MISTAKES

He who covers his sins will not prosper,
but whoever confesses and forsakes them
will have mercy.
PROVERBS 28:13 NKJV

Therefore let us approach the throne of grace
with boldness, so that we may receive mercy
and find grace to help us at the proper time.
HEBREWS 4:16 HCSB

But the mercy of the LORD is from everlasting
to everlasting upon them that fear him,
and his righteousness unto children's children.
PSALM 103:17 KJV

Be merciful, just as your Father is merciful.
LUKE 6:36 NIV

Therefore, if anyone is in Christ, he is a new creation;
old things have passed away;
behold, all things have become new.
2 CORINTHIANS 5:17 NKJV

52

MOTIVATING OTHERS

*The hearts of the wise make their mouths prudent,
and their lips promote instruction.*
PROVERBS 16:23 NIV

The best leaders find ways to motivate the people around them. How do they do it? With integrity, with clarity, with encouragement, and with hope.

Each day provides countless opportunities to encourage family, friends, and coworkers by praising their good works and acknowledging their accomplishments. When we do, we spread seeds of optimism and hope in a world that needs both.

In his letter to the Ephesians, Paul writes, "Do not let any unwholesome talk come out of your mouths, but only what is helpful for building others up according to their needs, that it may benefit those who listen" (4:29 NIV). These words remind us that when we choose our words carefully and well, we honor the One who gave His life for us.

*Leaders become great, not because of their power,
but because of their ability to empower others.*
JOHN MAXWELL

GOD'S PROMISES
ABOUT MOTIVATING OTHERS

A word spoken at the right time
is like golden apples on a silver tray.
PROVERBS 25:11 HCSB

Now finally, all of you should be like-minded
and sympathetic, should love believers,
and be compassionate and humble.
1 PETER 3:8 HCSB

But encourage one another day after day,
as long as it is still called "Today," so that none of you
will be hardened by the deceitfulness of sin.
HEBREWS 3:13 NASB

Therefore encourage one another and build
each other up as you are already doing.
1 THESSALONIANS 5:11 HCSB

Let the words of my mouth and the meditation
of my heart be acceptable in Your sight,
O LORD, my strength and my Redeemer.
PSALM 19:14 NKJV

53

OBEDIENCE

Now by this we know that we know Him,
if we keep His commandments.
1 JOHN 2:3 NKJV

Leaders expect obedience from their followers. And God expects no less from us. His instructions, which are contained in the Holy Bible, are given for our own benefit. When we obey God's commandments and listen carefully to the conscience He has placed in our hearts, we are secure. But if we disobey our Creator, if we choose to ignore the teachings and the warnings of His Word, we do so at great peril.

Billy Graham offered this warning: "The Bible teaches that when we turn our backs on God and choose to disregard His moral laws there are inevitable consequences." These words serve as a powerful reminder that, as Christians, we are called to take God's promises seriously and to live in accordance with His teachings.

God gave us His commandments for a reason: so that we might obey them and be blessed. Yet we live in a world that presents us with countless temptations to stray far from His path. It is our responsibility to resist those temptations with vigor. Obedience isn't just the best way to experience the full measure of God's blessings; it's the only way.

*One act of obedience is better than
one hundred sermons.*
DIETRICH BONHOEFFER

GOD'S PROMISES
ABOUT OBEDIENCE

We must obey God rather than men.
ACTS 5:29 NASB

*Teach me, O LORD, the way of Your statutes,
and I shall observe it to the end.*
PSALM 119:33 NASB

*Trust in the LORD with all your heart,
and lean not on your own understanding;
in all your ways acknowledge Him,
and He shall direct your paths.*
PROVERBS 3:5–6 NKJV

*Praise the LORD! Happy are those who respect
the LORD, who want what he commands.*
PSALM 112:1 NCV

*But prove yourselves doers of the word,
and not merely hearers who delude themselves.*
JAMES 1:22 NASB

54

OPPORTUNITIES

Remember ye not the former things, neither consider the things of old. Behold, I will do a new thing.
ISAIAH 43:18–19 KJV

Savvy leaders are constantly searching for opportunities, and not surprisingly, they often find what they're looking for.

As you consider the trajectory of your career—and as you consider your opportunities for leadership—do you see possibilities, opportunities, and blessings from above? Or do you focus on stumbling blocks?

If you're consistently looking for opportunities, you'll discover that opportunities have a way of turning up in the most unexpected places. But, if you've acquired the unfortunate habit of looking for problems instead of possibilities, you'll find that troubles have a way of turning up in unexpected places, too.

Since you're likely to find what you're looking for, why not look for opportunities? They're out there. And the rest is up to you.

We are all faced with a series of great opportunities brilliantly disguised as impossible situations.

CHARLES SWINDOLL

GOD'S PROMISES
ABOUT OPPORTUNITIES

*But as it is written: What eye did not see
and ear did not hear, and what never
entered the human mind—God prepared
this for those who love Him.*
1 CORINTHIANS 2:9 HCSB

*Whenever we have the opportunity,
we should do good to everyone—
especially to those in the family of faith.*
GALATIANS 6:10 NLT

*I can do all things through Christ
which strengtheneth me.*
PHILIPPIANS 4:13 KJV

I remind you to fan into flame the gift of God.
2 TIMOTHY 1:6 NIV

*But those who wait on the LORD
Shall renew their strength;
They shall mount up
with wings like eagles,
They shall run and not be weary,
They shall walk and not faint.*
ISAIAH 40:31 NKJV

55

OPTIMISM

The LORD is my light and my salvation—
whom should I fear? The LORD is the stronghold
of my life—of whom should I be afraid?
PSALM 27:1 HCSB

Are you a passionate Christian who expects God to do big things in your life and in the lives of those around you? If you're a thinking Christian, you have every reason to be confident about your future here on earth and your eternal future in heaven. But sometimes you may find yourself caught up in the inevitable complications of everyday living. When you find yourself fretting about the inevitable ups and downs of life here on earth, it's time to slow down, collect yourself, refocus your thoughts, and count your blessings.

God has made promises to you, and He will most certainly keep every one of them. So you have every reason to be an optimist and no legitimate reason to ever abandon hope.

Today, trust your hopes, not your fears. And while you're at it, take time to celebrate God's blessings. His gifts are too numerous to calculate and too glorious to imagine. But it never hurts to try.

Two types of voices command your attention today.
Negative ones fill your mind with doubt, bitterness,
and fear. Positive ones purvey hope and strength.
Which one will you choose to heed?

Max Lucado

GOD'S PROMISES ABOUT OPTIMISM

Make me to hear joy and gladness.

Psalm 51:8 KJV

But if we look forward to something we don't yet have,
we must wait patiently and confidently.

Romans 8:25 NLT

"I say this because I know what I am planning
for you," says the Lord. "I have good plans
for you, not plans to hurt you.
I will give you hope and a good future."

Jeremiah 29:11 NCV

This hope we have as an anchor of the soul,
a hope both sure and steadfast.

Hebrews 6:19 NASB

Let us hold on to the confession of our hope without
wavering, for He who promised is faithful.

Hebrews 10:23 HCSB

56

PAST

Do not remember the former things, nor consider the things of old. Behold, I will do a new thing.
ISAIAH 43:18–19 NKJV

As a Christian leader, you should learn from the past, but you shouldn't live there. But sometimes that's easier said than done. Yesterday's blunders are hard to forget, and past disappointments will sidetrack us if we let them.

Since we can't change the pains and disappointments of the past, why do so many of us insist upon replaying them over and over again in our minds? Perhaps it's because we can't find it in our hearts to forgive the people who have hurt us. Being mere mortals, we seek revenge, not reconciliation, and we harbor hatred in our hearts, sometimes for decades.

Reinhold Niebuhr composed a simple verse that came to be known as the Serenity Prayer: "God, grant me the serenity to accept the things I cannot change, the courage to change the things I can, and the wisdom to know the difference." Obviously we cannot change the past. It is what it was and forever will be. The present, of course, is a different matter.

Today is filled with opportunities to lead, to live, to love, to work, to play, and to celebrate life. If we sincerely wish to build a better tomorrow, we can start building it today, in the present moment.

So, if you've endured a difficult past, accept it, learn from it, and forgive everybody, including yourself. Once you've made peace with your past, don't spend too much time there. Instead, live in the precious present, where opportunities abound and change is still possible.

It is no use to pray for the old days;
stand square where you are and make
the present better than any past has been.
OSWALD CHAMBERS

GOD'S PROMISES ABOUT THE PAST

One thing I do, forgetting those things which are behind and reaching forward to those things which are ahead, I press toward the goal for the prize of the upward call of God in Christ Jesus.
PHILIPPIANS 3:13–14 NKJV

Have mercy on me, O God, according to your unfailing love; according to your great compassion blot out my transgressions. Wash away all my iniquity and cleanse me from my sin.
PSALM 51:1–2 NIV

Your old sinful self has died,
and your new life is kept with Christ in God.
COLOSSIANS 3:3 NCV

57

PATIENCE

A person's wisdom yields patience;
it is to one's glory to overlook an offense.
PROVERBS 19:11 NIV

Time and again, the Bible promises us that patience is its own reward, but not its only reward. Yet we human beings are, by nature, an impatient lot. We know what we want and we know when we want it: right now!

We live in an imperfect world inhabited by imperfect family members, imperfect friends, imperfect acquaintances, imperfect coworkers, and imperfect strangers. Sometimes we inherit troubles from these imperfect people, and sometimes we create troubles for ourselves. In either case, what's required is patience: patience for other people's shortcomings as well as our own.

Proverbs 16:32 teaches, "Better to be patient than powerful; better to have self-control than to conquer a city" (NLT). But for most of us, waiting patiently is hard. We are fallible beings who want things today, not tomorrow. Still, God instructs us to be patient and that's what we must do. It's the peaceful way to live.

Some of your greatest blessings come with patience.
WARREN WIERSBE

GOD'S PROMISES
ABOUT PATIENCE

*Patience of spirit is better than
haughtiness of spirit.*
ECCLESIASTES 7:8 NASB

*But if we hope for what we do not yet have,
we wait for it patiently.*
ROMANS 8:25 NIV

*Be joyful in hope, patient in affliction,
faithful in prayer.*
ROMANS 12:12 NIV

*The LORD is good to those who
depend on him, to those who search for him.
So it is good to wait quietly
for salvation from the LORD.*
LAMENTATIONS 3:25–26 NLT

58

PERSEVERANCE

Let us not become weary in doing good,
for at the proper time we will
reap a harvest if we do not give up.
GALATIANS 6:9 NIV

Occasionally good things happen with little or no effort. Somebody wins the lottery, or inherits a fortune, or stumbles onto a financial bonanza by being at the right place at the right time. But more often than not, good things happen to people who work hard, and keep working hard, when just about everybody else has gone home or given up.

Calvin Coolidge observed, "Nothing in the world can take the place of persistence. Talent will not; genius will not; education will not. Persistence and determination alone are omnipotent." And President Coolidge was right. Perseverance pays.

Every marathon has a finish line, and so does yours. So keep putting one foot in front of the other, pray for strength, and don't give up. Whether you realize it or not, you're up to the challenge if you persevere. And with God's help, that's exactly what you'll do.

The Christian's journey through life
isn't a sprint but a marathon.
BILLY GRAHAM

GOD'S PROMISES
ABOUT PERSEVERANCE

But as for you, be strong; don't be discouraged,
for your work has a reward.
2 CHRONICLES 15:7 HCSB

We are hard-pressed on every side, yet not crushed;
we are perplexed, but not in despair.
2 CORINTHIANS 4:8 NKJV

Finishing is better than starting.
Patience is better than pride.
ECCLESIASTES 7:8 NLT

For you have need of endurance,
so that when you have done the will of God,
you may receive what was promised.
HEBREWS 10:36 NASB

So let us run the race that is before us
and never give up. We should remove from
our lives anything that would get in the way
and the sin that so easily holds us back.
HEBREWS 12:1 NCV

59

PLANNING

The wise see danger ahead and avoid it,
but fools keep going and get into trouble.
PROVERBS 22:3 NCV

If you're like most people, you probably have some sort of informal master plan for your life, a general idea of where you want to go and how you want to get there. But sometimes informal plans aren't enough. Savvy leaders know—and the Bible makes it clear—that careful planning pays impressive dividends, while impulsive decision making often does not.

Are you willing to plan for your future and work for it? And are you willing to make God a participating partner in every aspect of that plan? If so, you can be sure that the Lord will give you strength and guide your path. So, pray about your plans, commit them to writing, and commit them to God. Then, get busy, get excited, and get ready to reap the bountiful harvest that He most certainly has in store.

It is important to set goals because
if you do not have a plan, a goal, a direction,
a purpose, and a focus, you are not going
to accomplish anything for the glory of God.
BILL BRIGHT

GOD'S PROMISES
ABOUT PLANNING

A noble person plans noble things;
he stands up for noble causes.
ISAIAH 32:8 HCSB

Let your eyes look forward;
fix your gaze straight ahead.
PROVERBS 4:25 HCSB

A wise person will listen and increase his learning,
and a discerning man will obtain guidance.
PROVERBS 1:5 HCSB

So prepare your minds for action
and exercise self-control.
Put all your hope in the gracious salvation
that will come to you when
Jesus Christ is revealed to the world.
1 PETER 1:13 NLT

Trust in the LORD with all your heart, and lean not
on your own understanding; in all your ways
acknowledge Him, and He shall direct your paths.
PROVERBS 3:5–6 NKJV

60

POPULARITY

For am I now trying to win the favor of people,
or God? Or am I striving to please people?
If I were still trying to please people,
I would not be a slave of Christ.
GALATIANS 1:10 HCSB

It feels good to be popular. That's why so many of us invest so much time, energy, and personal capital trying to gain the approval of our peers. But oftentimes, in our efforts to gain earthly approval, we make spiritual sacrifices. Big mistake.

It always pays to put God first and keep Him there. When we do, our other priorities tend to fall into place. But, when we focus too intently on worldly pursuits, we suffer.

So today, as you make preparations for the day ahead, think less about pleasing people and more about pleasing your Creator. It's the best way—and the safest way—to live.

Those who follow the crowd usually get lost in it.
I don't know all the keys to success, but one key
to failure is to try to please everyone.
RICK WARREN

GOD'S PROMISES
ABOUT POPULARITY

The fear of man is a snare, but the one
who trusts in the LORD is protected.
PROVERBS 29:25 HCSB

It is better to take refuge in the LORD
than to trust in man.
PSALM 118:8 HCSB

My son, if sinners entice you,
don't be persuaded.
PROVERBS 1:10 HCSB

Keep your eyes focused on what is right.
Keep looking straight ahead to what is good.
PROVERBS 4:25 ICB

Do not be unequally yoked together
with unbelievers. For what fellowship
has righteousness with lawlessness?
And what communion has light with darkness?
2 CORINTHIANS 6:14 NKJV

61

POSSIBILITIES

But Jesus looked at them and said to them,
"With men this is impossible, but with God
all things are possible."
MATTHEW 19:26 NKJV

The world is brimming with possibilities. And the same can be said for *your* world. You possess a unique assortment of talents and opportunities on loan from the Creator.

God has put you in a particular place at a specific time of His choosing. He has an assignment that is uniquely yours, tasks that are specially intended just for you. And whether you know it or not, He's equipped you with everything you need to fulfill His purpose and achieve His plans.

The next time you find yourself fretting about the future or worrying about things that may never come to pass, refocus your thoughts on the positive aspects of life here on earth and life eternal in heaven. And while you're at it, remember that with God all things are possible. When you let Him take over, there's simply no limit to the things that the two of you, working together, can accomplish.

When God is involved, anything can happen. Be open.
Stay that way. God has a beautiful way of bringing
good vibrations out of broken chords.
CHARLES SWINDOLL

GOD'S PROMISES
ABOUT POSSIBILITIES

I can do all things through Christ
which strengtheneth me.
PHILIPPIANS 4:13 KJV

Jesus said to him, "If you can believe,
all things are possible to him who believes."
MARK 9:23 NKJV

The things which are impossible
with men are possible with God.
LUKE 18:27 KJV

Therefore we do not lose heart.
Even though our outward man is perishing,
yet the inward man is being renewed day by day.
2 CORINTHIANS 4:16 NKJV

Is anything too hard for the LORD?
GENESIS 18:14 KJV

62

PRAYER

Rejoice always, pray without ceasing,
in everything give thanks; for this is the will of God
in Christ Jesus for you.
1 THESSALONIANS 5:16–18 NKJV

Wise Christian leaders understand the power of prayer, and they never make an important decision without consulting God first. So, here's a question that was first posed by Corrie ten Boom: "Is prayer your steering wheel or your spare tire?"

Prayer is a powerful tool that you can use to change your world and change yourself. God hears every prayer and responds in His own way and according to His own timetable. When you make a habit of consulting Him about everything, He'll guide you along a path of His choosing, which, by the way, is the path you should take. And when you petition Him for strength, He'll give you the courage to face any problem and the power to meet any challenge. So today, instead of turning things over in your mind, turn them over to God in prayer. Take your concerns to the Lord and leave them there. Your heavenly Father is listening, and He wants to hear from you. Now.

Prayer is of transcendent importance.
Prayer is the mightiest agent to advance God's work.
Praying hearts and hands only can do God's work.
Prayer succeeds when all else fails.
E. M. BOUNDS

GOD'S PROMISES
ABOUT PRAYER

I desire therefore that the men pray everywhere,
lifting up holy hands, without wrath and doubting.
1 TIMOTHY 2:8 NKJV

Confess your trespasses to one another, and pray
for one another, that you may be healed. The effective,
fervent prayer of a righteous man avails much.
JAMES 5:16 NKJV

And whenever you stand praying, if you have anything
against anyone, forgive him, so that your Father in
heaven will also forgive you your wrongdoing.
MARK 11:25 HCSB

Ask, and it will be given to you; seek,
and you will find; knock, and it will be opened
to you. For everyone who asks receives, and he who
seeks finds, and to him who knocks it will be opened.
MATTHEW 7:7-8 NASB

63

PRIORITIES

*Therefore, whether you eat or drink,
or whatever you do, do everything for God's glory.*
1 CORINTHIANS 10:31 HCSB

Part of every leader's job is establishing priorities: priorities for his teammates and priorities for himself. What are your priorities for the coming day and the coming year? Will you focus on your organization, your family, your finances, your health? All these things are important, of course, but God asks you to focus on something entirely different; God asks that you focus, not on yourself or your world, but on Him.

Every morning, when you rise from bed and prepare for the coming day, the world attempts to arrange your priorities, to fill your schedule, and to crowd out God. The world says you're too busy to pray, too busy to study God's Word, and too busy to thank Him for His gifts. The world says you need noise instead of silence, entertainment instead of contemplation, constant contact instead of solitude. And the world says that you'll stay on the right track if you simply do enough and acquire enough. But God begs to differ. He asks that you quiet yourself each day and listen to Him. And He promises that when you listen, He will lead.

So, as you think about the things in your life that

really matter—and as you establish priorities for the coming day—remember to let God lead the way. And while you're at it, remember that the things that matter most are always the things that have eternal consequences.

You will not be in heaven two seconds before you cry out, Why did I place so much importance on things that were so temporary? What was I thinking? Why did I waste so much time, energy, and concern on what wasn't going to last?
RICK WARREN

GOD'S PROMISES
ABOUT PRIORITIES

Trust in the LORD with all your heart and lean not on your own understanding.
PROVERBS 3:5 NIV

Make yourself an example of good works with integrity and dignity in your teaching.
TITUS 2:7 HCSB

But prove yourselves doers of the word, and not merely hearers who delude themselves.
JAMES 1:22 NASB

For where your treasure is, there your heart will be also.
LUKE 12:34 HCSB

64

PROBLEMS AND PROBLEM SOLVING

People who do what is right may have many problems,
but the LORD will solve them all.
PSALM 34:19 NCV

Savvy leaders recognize problems and address them as quickly as possible. But sometimes those problems may seem too big to tackle. They are not. With God, all things are possible.

On those cloudy days when Old Man Trouble pays a visit and problems seem to be popping up everywhere, there exists a source from which we can draw perspective and courage. That source, of course, is our Creator. When we turn our troubles over to Him, we find that He is sufficient to meet our needs.

So, the next time you feel discouraged, slow down long enough to have a serious talk with your Creator. Pray for guidance, pray for strength, and pray for the wisdom to trust your heavenly Father. Your troubles are temporary; His love is not.

Each problem is a God-appointed instructor.
CHARLES SWINDOLL

GOD'S PROMISES
ABOUT PROBLEM SOLVING

Consider it pure joy, my brothers and sisters,
whenever you face trials of many kinds,
because you know that the testing
of your faith develops perseverance.
JAMES 1:2–3 NIV

We also have joy with our troubles, because we know
that these troubles produce patience. And patience
produces character, and character produces hope.
ROMANS 5:3–4 NCV

Trust the LORD your God with all your heart
and lean not on your own understanding;
in all your ways acknowledge him,
and he will make your paths straight.
PROVERBS 3:5–6 NIV

We are pressured in every way but not crushed;
we are perplexed but not in despair.
2 CORINTHIANS 4:8 HCSB

I have learned in whatever state I am, to be content.
PHILIPPIANS 4:11 NKJV

65

PURPOSE

We have also received an inheritance in Him,
predestined according to the purpose
of the One who works out everything
in agreement with the decision of His will.
EPHESIANS 1:11 HCSB

Great leaders don't do things by accident, and neither does God. He didn't put you here by chance. He didn't deliver you to your particular place, at this particular time, with your particular set of talents and opportunities, on a whim. The Lord has a plan, a one-of-a-kind mission designed especially for you. Discovering that plan may take time. But if you keep asking God for guidance, He'll lead along a path of His choosing and give you every tool you need to fulfill His will.

Of course, you'll probably encounter a few impediments as you attempt to discover the exact nature of God's purpose for your life. And you may travel down a few dead ends along the way. But if you keep searching, and if you genuinely seek the Lord's guidance, He'll reveal His plans at a time and place of His own choosing.

Today and every day, God is beckoning you to hear His voice and follow His plan for your life. When you listen—and when you answer His call—you'll be amazed at the wonderful things that an all-knowing, all-powerful God can do.

*The easiest way to discover the purpose of
an invention is to ask the creator of it. The same
is true for discovering your life's purpose: Ask God.*

RICK WARREN

GOD'S PROMISES
ABOUT PURPOSE

*Whether you eat or drink or whatever you do,
do it all for the glory of God.*

1 CORINTHIANS 10:31 NLT

*For we are God's co-workers.
You are God's field, God's building.*

1 CORINTHIANS 3:9 HCSB

*For we are His creation, created in Christ Jesus
for good works, which God prepared ahead
of time so that we should walk in them.*

EPHESIANS 2:10 HCSB

*We must do the works of Him who sent Me while
it is day. Night is coming when no one can work.*

JOHN 9:4 HCSB

*And whatever you do, do it heartily,
as to the Lord and not to men.*

COLOSSIANS 3:23 NKJV

66

RESPONSIBILITY

So then, each of us will give
an account of himself to God.
ROMANS 14:12 HCSB

God's Word encourages us to take responsibility for our actions, but the world tempts us to do otherwise. The media tries to convince us that we're "victims" of our upbringing, our government, our economic strata, or our circumstances, thus ignoring the countless blessings—and the gift of free will— that God has given each of us.

Who's responsible for your behavior? God's Word says that you are. If you obey His instructions and follow His Son, you'll be blessed in countless ways. But if you ignore the Lord's teachings, you must eventually bear the consequences of those irresponsible decisions.

Today and every day, as you make decisions about the things you'll say and do, remember who's responsible. And if you make a mistake, admit it, learn from it, and move on. The blame game has no winners; don't play.

No man is fit to command another
that cannot command himself.
WILLIAM PENN

GOD'S PROMISES
ABOUT RESPONSIBILITY

But each person should examine his own work,
and then he will have a reason for boasting
in himself alone, and not in respect to someone else.
For each person will have to carry his own load.
GALATIANS 6:4–5 HCSB

Better to be patient than powerful;
better to have self-control than to conquer a city.
PROVERBS 16:32 NLT

Then He said to His disciples,
"The harvest is abundant, but the workers are few."
MATTHEW 9:37 HCSB

By their fruits ye shall know them.
MATTHEW 7:20 KJV

We must do the works of Him who sent Me
while it is day. Night is coming when no one can work.
JOHN 9:4 HCSB

67

RISK

The prudent see danger and takes refuge,
but the simple keep going and pay the penalty.
PROVERBS 22:3 NIV

All the principles that you'll ever need to manage risk and live wisely can be found in a single book: the Bible. God's Word guides us along a path that leads to abundance and eternal life. When we embrace Biblical teachings and follow God's Son, we're protected. But when we wander from His path, we inevitably suffer the consequences of our mistaken priorities.

In theory, all of us would prefer to be wise, but not all of us are willing to make the sacrifices that are required to gain real wisdom. To become wise, we must do more than spout platitudes, recite verses, or repeat aphorisms. We must not only speak wisely; we must live wisely. We must not only learn the lessons of the Christian life; we must live by them.

Today, as you think about the best way to live and to lead, remember that God's wisdom can be found in a book that's already on your bookshelf: His Book. Read, heed, and lead accordingly.

You'll never reach second base
if you keep one foot on first.
VERNON LAW

GOD'S PROMISES
ABOUT RISK

Enthusiasm without knowledge is no good;
haste makes mistakes.
PROVERBS 19:2 NLT

Spend time with the wise and you will become wise,
but the friends of fools will suffer.
PROVERBS 13:20 NCV

The LORD detests the proud;
they will surely be punished.
PROVERBS 16:5 NLT

But the noble man makes noble plans,
and by noble deeds he stands.
ISAIAH 32:8 NIV

Commit your actions to the LORD,
and your plans will succeed.
PROVERBS 16:3 NLT

68

SERVICE AND
SERVING GOD

He who is greatest among you shall be your servant.
And whoever exalts himself will be humbled,
and he who humbles himself will be exalted.
MATTHEW 23:11–12 NKJV

Jesus was a servant-leader, and leaders who seek to follow in His footsteps must be servants, too. But the world tries to convince us otherwise by promoting a get-ahead-at-any-cost mentality. Christian leaders, on the other hand, promote a lend-a-helping-hand mentality in the workplace and beyond.

Everywhere we look, the needs are great. Whether here at home or halfway around the globe, so many people are enduring difficult circumstances. They need help, and as Christians, we are instructed to serve them.

Jesus came to this world not to conquer but to serve. We must do likewise by helping those who cannot help themselves. When we do, our lives will be blessed by the One who first served us.

Thinking of and serving with others can be
an antidote to negative and unhealthy introspection.
BILLY GRAHAM

GOD'S PROMISES
ABOUT SERVICE

Shepherd God's flock, for whom you are responsible.
Watch over them because you want to,
not because you are forced. That is how God wants it.
Do it because you are happy to serve.
1 PETER 5:2 NCV

As each one has received a gift, minister it to one
another, as good stewards of the manifold grace of God.
1 PETER 4:10 NKJV

Blessed are those servants, whom the lord
when he cometh shall find watching.
LUKE 12:37 KJV

Assuredly, I say to you, inasmuch as you did it to one
of the least of these My brethren, you did it to Me.
MATTHEW 25:40 NKJV

Even so faith, if it hath not works,
is dead, being alone.
JAMES 2:17 KJV

69

STRENGTH

He gives strength to the weary, and to him
who lacks might He increases power.
ISAIAH 40:29 NASB

It takes energy to be a great leader. So, where do you turn for strength when you're weary or worried? The medicine cabinet? The gym? The health food store? These places may offer a temporary energy boost, but the best place to find strength and solace isn't down the hall or at the mall; it's as near as your next breath. The best source of strength is God.

God's love for you never changes, and neither does His support. From the cradle to the grave, He has promised to give you the strength to meet the challenges of life. He has promised to guide you and protect you if you let Him. But He also expects you to do your part.

Today provides yet another opportunity to partake in the strength that only God can provide. You do so by attuning your heart to Him through prayer, obedience, and trust. Life can be challenging, but fear not. Whatever your challenge, God can give you the strength to face it and to overcome it. Let Him.

Strive in prayer; let faith fill your heart so will you
be strong in the Lord, and in the power of His might.
ANDREW MURRAY

GOD'S PROMISES
ABOUT STRENGTH

The LORD is my strength and my song;
He has become my salvation.
EXODUS 15:2 HCSB

My grace is sufficient for you,
for my power is made perfect in weakness.
2 CORINTHIANS 12:9 NIV

Have faith in the LORD your God,
and you will stand strong. Have faith
in his prophets, and you will succeed.
2 CHRONICLES 20:20 NCV

Be strong and brave, and do the work.
Don't be afraid or discouraged, for the LORD God,
my God, is with you. He will not fail you or leave you.
1 CHRONICLES 28:20 HCSB

I can do all things through Christ who strengthens me.
PHILIPPIANS 4:13 NKJV

70

STRESS AND REST

Come unto me, all ye that labour
and are heavy laden, and I will give you rest.
MATTHEW 11:28 KJV

You inhabit an interconnected world that never slows down and never shuts off. The world tempts you to stay up late watching the news, or surfing the Internet, or checking out social media, or gaming, or doing countless other activities that gobble up your time and distract you from more important tasks. But too much late-night screen time robs you of something you need very badly: sleep.

Are you going to bed at a reasonable hour and sleeping through the night? If so, you're both wise and blessed. But if you're staying up late with your eyes glued to a screen, you're putting your long-term health at risk. And you're probably wasting time, too.

So the next time you're tempted to engage in late-night time wasting, resist the temptation. Instead, turn your thoughts and prayers to God. And when you're finished, turn off the lights and go to bed. You need rest more than you need entertainment.

Beware of having so much to do
that you really do nothing at all.
C. H. SPURGEON

GOD'S PROMISES
ABOUT STRESS AND REST

And the peace of God, which transcends
all understanding, will guard your hearts
and your minds in Christ Jesus.
PHILIPPIANS 4:7 NIV

I find rest in God; only he gives me hope.
PSALM 62:5 NCV

Peace I leave with you; My peace I give to you;
not as the world gives do I give to you.
Do not let your heart be troubled, nor let it be fearful.
JOHN 14:27 NASB

You, LORD, give true peace to those who
depend on you, because they trust you.
ISAIAH 26:3 NCV

Live peaceful and quiet lives in
all godliness and holiness.
1 TIMOTHY 2:2 NIV

71

THANKSGIVING

Enter into His gates with thanksgiving, and into His courts with praise. Be thankful to Him, and bless His name. For the LORD is good; His mercy is everlasting, and His truth endures to all generations.
PSALM 100:4–5 NKJV

When we consider God's blessings and the sacrifices of His Son, just how thankful should we be? Should we praise our Creator once a day? Are two prayers enough? Is it sufficient that we thank our heavenly Father at mealtimes and bedtimes? The answer, of course, is no. When we consider how richly we have been blessed, now and forever—and when we consider the price Christ paid on the cross—it becomes clear that we should offer many prayers of thanks throughout the day. But all too often, amid the hustle of daily life, we forget to pause and praise the Giver of all good gifts.

Our lives expand or contract in proportion to our gratitude. When we are appropriately grateful for God's countless blessings, we experience His peace. But if we ignore His gifts, we invite stress, anxiety, and sadness into our lives.

Throughout this day, pause and say silent prayers of thanks. When you do, you'll discover that a grateful heart reaps countless blessings that a hardened heart will never know.

The Bible tells us that whenever we come before God,
whatever our purpose or prayer request,
we are always to come with a thankful heart.
DAVID JEREMIAH

GOD'S PROMISES
ABOUT THANKSGIVING

And whatever you do, in word or in deed,
do everything in the name of the Lord Jesus,
giving thanks to God the Father through Him.
COLOSSIANS 3:17 HCSB

Rejoice always, pray without ceasing,
in everything give thanks; for this is
the will of God in Christ Jesus for you.
1 THESSALONIANS 5:16–18 NKJV

Surely the righteous shall give thanks to Your name;
the upright shall dwell in Your presence.
PSALM 140:13 NKJV

I will thank Yahweh with all my heart; I will declare
all Your wonderful works. I will rejoice and boast
about You; I will sing about Your name, Most High.
PSALM 9:1–2 HCSB

Thanks be to God for His indescribable gift.
2 CORINTHIANS 9:15 HCSB

72

THOUGHTS

*Set your mind on things above,
not on things on the earth.*
COLOSSIANS 3:2 NKJV

Because we are human, we are always busy with our thoughts. We simply can't help ourselves. Our brains never shut off, and even while we're sleeping, we mull things over in our minds. The question is not *if* we will think; the question is *how* we will think and *what* we will think about.

All too often we allow the worries of everyday life to overwhelm our thoughts and cloud our vision. What's needed is clearer perspective, renewed faith, and a different focus.

When we focus on the frustrations of today or the uncertainties of tomorrow, we rob ourselves of peace in the present moment. But when we direct our thoughts in more positive directions, we rob our worries of the power to tyrannize us.

You will make your life better when you focus your thoughts on your blessings, not your misfortunes. So do yourself, your family, your friends, and your coworkers a favor: Learn to think optimistically about the world you live in and the life you lead. Then prepare yourself for the blessings that good thoughts will bring.

*Your life today is a result of your thinking
yesterday. Your life tomorrow will
be determined by what you think today.*
JOHN MAXWELL

GOD'S PROMISES
ABOUT THOUGHTS

*The peace of God, which surpasses
all understanding, will guard your hearts
and minds through Christ Jesus.*
PHILIPPIANS 4:7 NKJV

*Finally, brothers and sisters, whatever is true,
whatever is noble, whatever is right, whatever is pure,
whatever is lovely, whatever is admirable—
if anything is excellent or praiseworthy—
think about such things.*
PHILIPPIANS 4:8 NIV

*Guard your heart above all else,
for it is the source of life.*
PROVERBS 4:23 HCSB

*And do not be conformed to this world,
but be transformed by the renewing of your mind,
so that you may prove what the will of God is,
that which is good and acceptable and perfect.*
ROMANS 12:2 NASB

73

VALUES

The righteousness of the blameless clears his path,
but the wicked person will fall because of his wickedness.
PROVERBS 11:5 HCSB

Great leaders know where they stand and what they stand for. They know the values that matter most, and they live by them. And they communicate those values to their coworkers and teammates.

God's Word teaches us how to live; it tells us what to do and what not to do. As Christians we are called to walk with God's Son and to obey God's commandments. But we live in a world that presents us with many temptations, each of which has the potential to distract us or destroy us.

Charles Swindoll correctly observed, "Nothing speaks louder or more powerfully than a life of integrity." Wise leaders agree. So, as you establish the set of values that you'll live by—and lead by—make the Bible your guidebook. When you do, you'll be protected and you'll be blessed.

When you live in the light of eternity,
your values change.
RICK WARREN

GOD'S PROMISES
ABOUT VALUES

So I strive always to keep my conscience
clear before God and man.
ACTS 24:16 NIV

Let us come near to God with a sincere heart
and a sure faith, because we have been made free
from a guilty conscience, and our bodies
have been washed with pure water.
HEBREWS 10:22 NCV

If then you were raised with Christ,
seek those things which are above, where Christ is,
sitting at the right hand of God. Set your mind
on things above, not on things on the earth.
COLOSSIANS 3:1–2 NKJV

Do not conform to the pattern of this world,
but be transformed by the renewing of your mind.
Then you will be able to test and approve what God's
will is—his good, pleasing and perfect will.
ROMANS 12:2 NIV

The integrity of the upright guides them,
but the perversity of the treacherous destroys them.
PROVERBS 11:3 HCSB

74

WISDOM AND UNDERSTANDING

The fear of the LORD is the beginning of knowledge,
but fools despise wisdom and instruction.
PROVERBS 1:7 NKJV

What makes a wise leader? Training, of course. And experience. And judgment. And common sense. But all these things, valuable though they may be, aren't enough. Genuine wisdom begins with God's Word.

Savvy leaders know that the search for wisdom is a lifelong journey. We should continue to read, to watch, to test our assumptions, and to learn new things as long as we live. But it's not enough to learn new things or to memorize the great Biblical truths; we must also live by them.

So, what will you learn today? Will you take time to feed your mind and fill your heart? And will you study the guidebook that God has given you? Hopefully so, because His plans and His promises are waiting for you there, inside the covers of a book like no other: His book. It contains the essential wisdom you'll need to navigate the seas of life and land safely on that distant shore.

The more wisdom enters our hearts, the more we will
be able to trust our hearts in difficult situations.
JOHN ELDREDGE

GOD'S PROMISES ABOUT WISDOM AND UNDERSTANDING

Get wisdom—how much better it is than gold!
And get understanding—it is preferable to silver.
PROVERBS 16:16 HCSB

But the wisdom that is from above is first pure, then
peaceable, gentle, willing to yield, full of mercy and
good fruits, without partiality and without hypocrisy.
JAMES 3:17 NKJV

He that walketh with wise men shall be wise:
but a companion of fools shall be destroyed.
PROVERBS 13:20 KJV

But if any of you lacks wisdom, let him ask of God,
who gives to all generously and without reproach,
and it will be given to him.
JAMES 1:5 NASB

Who among you is wise and understanding?
Let him show by his good behavior his deeds
in the gentleness of wisdom.
JAMES 3:13 NASB

75

WORK

Whatever you do, do it enthusiastically,
as something done for the Lord and not for men.
COLOSSIANS 3:23 HCSB

Time and again, the Bible extols the value of hard work. In Proverbs we are instructed to take a lesson from a surprising source: ants. Ants are among nature's most industrious creatures. They do their work without supervision, hesitation, or complaint. We should do likewise, but oftentimes we don't. We're tempted to look for shortcuts (there aren't any), or we rely on luck (it happens, but we shouldn't depend on it). Meanwhile, the clock continues to tick, life continues to pass, and important work goes undone.

The book of Proverbs proclaims, "One who is slack in his work is brother to one who destroys" (18:9 NIV). And in his second letter to the Thessalonians, Paul writes, "If any would not work, neither should he eat" (3:10 KJV). In short, God has created a world in which labor is rewarded but laziness is not.

As you think about the way you lead and the way you work, please remember that God has big plans for you, and He's given you everything you need to fulfill His purpose. But He won't force His plans upon you, and He won't do all the work. He expects you to do your part. When you do, you'll earn the rewards He most certainly has in store.

Think of something you ought to do and go do it.
Heed not your feelings. Do your work.
George MacDonald

GOD'S PROMISES
ABOUT WORK

But this I say: He who sows sparingly
will also reap sparingly, and he who sows bountifully
will also reap bountifully.
2 Corinthians 9:6 NKJV

Be strong and courageous, and do the work.
Don't be afraid or discouraged, for the LORD God,
my God, is with you. He won't leave you or forsake you.
1 Chronicles 28:20 HCSB

The plans of hard-working people earn a profit,
but those who act too quickly become poor.
Proverbs 21:5 NCV

Do you see a man skilled in his work?
He will stand in the presence of kings.
Proverbs 22:29 HCSB

I must work the works of Him who sent Me while
it is day; the night is coming when no one can work.
John 9:4 NKJV

LIVE YOUR FAITH

Dear Friend,

This book was prayerfully crafted with you, the reader, in mind—every word, every sentence, every page—was thoughtfully written, designed, and packaged to encourage you...right where you are this very moment. At DaySpring, our vision is to see every person experience the life-changing message of God's love. So, as we worked through rough drafts, design changes, edits and details, we prayed for you to deeply experience His unfailing love, indescribable peace, and pure joy. It is our sincére hope that through these Truth-filled pages your heart will be blessed, knowing that God cares about you—your desires and disappointments, your challenges and dreams.

He knows. He cares. He loves you unconditionally.

BLESSINGS!
THE DAYSPRING BOOK TEAM

Additional copies of this book and
other DaySpring titles can be purchased
at fine bookstores everywhere.
Order online at <u>dayspring.com</u>
or
by phone at 1-877-751-4347